D1860210

BUDDHISM

ITS HISTORICAL THEORETICAL AND POPULAR ASPECTS

BUDDHISM

ITS HISTORICAL THEORETICAL AND POPULAR ASPECTS

IN THREE LECTURES

ERNEST J. EITEL

SECOND EDITION

GYAN

Published by

Gyan Publishing House
5, Ansari Road
Daryaganj, New Delhi-110002
Phone: 011-47034999, 9811692060
E-mail: books@gyanbooks.com

Distribution Network
gyanbooks.com
India, USA, Canada, UK, Australia, France

© Publisher

All rights reserved. No part of this work may be reproduced, stored, adapted, or transmitted in any form or by any means, electronic, mechanical, photocopying, micro-filming, recording or otherwise, or translated in any language, without the prior written permission of the copyright owner and the publisher.

ISBN : 978-81-212-3173-2 (PB)
First Published, London, 1873

2nd Impression 2020

Printed at: Gyan Press, Delhi.

The book is sold subject to the condition that it shall not, by way of trade or otherwise, be lent, resold, hired out, or otherwise circulated without the prior publisher's written consent.

Buddhism
Author: Ernest J. Eitel

PREFACE TO THE SECOND EDITION.

THE rapidity with which the first edition of these Lectures was exhausted and the favour with which the book was generally received by the public press, especially in China, encouraged the author to satisfy the continuing demand for it by a second edition.

A few corrections and alterations have been introduced here and there, but the form and substance of the book remain untouched.

HONGKONG, *July*, 1873.

PREFACE TO THE FIRST EDITION.

Two of the following essays on Buddhism formed part of a series of popular lectures, delivered in Union Church in the course of the winter 1870-71. To complete the plan laid down in the first essay, it was necessary to add a third, and the whole is herewith offered to the reader as a popular sketch of Buddhism, which is here viewed under its different aspects, as an event in history, as a system of doctrine, and as a popular religion. Considering the character of the audience before which these lectures were delivered, the author avoided as much as possible going into details, and confined his remarks to the more prominent features of Buddhism. Those who wish to make themselves further acquainted with this important religion may refer to the author's "Handbook for the Student of Chinese Buddhism; London, Trübner & Co., 1870," to which more painstaking work the present pamphlet may serve as a general introduction.

HONGKONG, *March*, 1871.

LECTURE THE FIRST.

BUDDHISM, AN EVENT IN HISTORY.

IT is with considerable hesitation, that I set out on this inquiry into the subject of Buddhism. Not as if I had given years of study to this particular religion, and yet failed to make myself familiar with its general characteristics and minute details. It is the magnitude and importance of the subject that appals me and in view of which I naturally feel distrustful of my own power to deal with that subject in a satisfactory and yet attractive manner.

Buddhism, I repeat, is a system of vast magnitude, for it embraces all the various branches of science, which our Western nations have been long accustomed to divide for separate study. It embodies in one living structure grand and peculiar views of physical science, refined and subtle theorems on abstract metaphysics, an edifice of fanciful mysticism, a most elaborate and far-reaching system of practical morality, and finally a church organisation as broad in its principles and as finely wrought in its most intricate network as any in the world.

All this is moreover combined and worked up in such a manner, that the essence and substance of the whole may be compressed into a few formulas and symbols, plain and suggestive enough to be grasped by the most simple-minded Asiatic, and yet so full of philosophic depth, as to provide rich food for years of meditation to the metaphysician, the poet, the mystic, and pleasant pasturage for the most fiery imagination of any poetical dreamer.

The magnitude of the subject, however, is but equalled by its importance. A system which takes its roots in the oldest code-book of Asiatic nations, in the Vêda, a theory which extracted and remodelled all the best ideas that were ever laid hold of by ancient Brahmanism, a religion which has not only managed to subsist for 2400 years, but which has succeeded to draw within the meshes of its own peculiar church-organization and to bring more or less under the influence of its own peculiar tenets more than four hundred millions of people, fully one third of the human race,—such a system, such a religion ought to have importance enough in our eyes to deserve something more than passing or passive attention.

The history of Eastern Asia is the history of Buddhism. But the conquests of Buddhism are not confined to Asia. This grand system of philosophic atheism, which discards from the universe the existence of a creating and overruling Deity and in its place deifies humanity, has, since the beginning of the present century, entered upon a course of conquest in the West, in Europe and America.

Atheistic philosophers, unconsciously attracted by the natural affinity, which draws together Atheists of all countries and ages, have during the last fifty years almost instinctively gone on sipping at the intoxicating cup of Buddhistic philosophy. The Germans Feuerbach and Schoppenhauer, the Frenchman Comte, the Englishman Lewis, the American Emerson, with hosts of others, have all drunk more or less of this sweet poison and taken as kindly as any Asiatic to this Buddhistic opium-pipe. But most of all that latest product of modern philosophy, the so-called system of positive religion, the school of Comte, with its religion of humanity, is but Buddhism adapted to modern civilisation, it is philosophic Buddhism in a slight disguise.

I mention these facts only, to claim the attention of my readers for the subject of these three lectures, being aware of the prejudices which deter people from a study so unpromising at first sight and uninviting as that of Buddhism. But to guide them through the vast labyrinth of Buddhistic literature and doctrines with something like method, I would divide the subject matter under discussion into three parts and treat Buddhism first as an event in history, secondly as a dogmatic system, and finally consider its aspects as a popular religion. I propose therefore to treat Buddhism in this first lecture as an event in the history of the world, to search for the hidden roots of the gigantic tree of knowledge under the boughs of which one third of the human race has flocked together. Let us watch its gradual growth through successive centuries, let us count the large branches it has sent forth in all directions and ascertain its present condition and extent.

But here, at the outset, we meet with the usual difficulty that obstructs the way of the historian who wants to get at the roots of events: they are hidden in complete darkness. There is such a network of fiction, romance, legend and truth lying around the early history of Buddhism, that it is an exceedingly difficult task to sift truth from fiction.

And yet these legends and myths ought not to be despised by the historian, ought not to be thrown aside as worthless rubbish. They are often very significant, a very master-key to many specific characteristics of after-developments, a rich ore of hidden wealth to him who patiently works through them and knows how to appreciate them with discerning caution.

I shall not ask my readers, however, to follow me through the tedious process of sifting out the truth from among the entangled mass of legends about the first origin of Buddhism. I will give them but the results of careful investigations and lightly sketch first the few historic data that crop out of the chaos of legend and fable, and then arrange the same according to the received tradition of the Buddhist church.

One thing is absolutely certain as regards the origin of Buddhism, and that is, that it first arose in India. All Buddhists of all countries point to India as the birthplace of their religion, and strange to say all Buddhists, North and South, are equally unanimous in singling out one and the same city, the city of Benares, as the first headquarters of early Buddhism.

Again, there is perfect unanimity as to the name of the great founder of the present Buddhist church, one Shâkyamuni Gâutama Buddha. As to the time when this man lived or died, great confusion prevails, traditions of one and the same country often contradicting each other. One Chinese account, for instance, places it as early as 949 B.C., another, more modest, names the year 688 B.C., whilst the Buddhists of Ceylon fixed upon the year 543 B.C. As the latter date is confirmed by the lately discovered chronicle of Cashmere, and as other considerations, inscriptions and coins for instance, point to the same century, it is now generally agreed upon among European scholars that the year 543 B.C. is most probably the year in which Shâkyamuni Gâutama Buddha died.

Regarding the private history of this truly great man very little can be ascertained with perfect certainty,—beyond the following facts: that he claimed to be of royal descent, that, dissatisfied with Brahmanism, he left house and home, tried first to find peace in the most austere asceticism, but finally emerged, disentangling himself from the social trammels of caste and all sectarian doctrines, teaching voluntary poverty and celibacy, and erecting on the basis of all existing religions a grand system, the chief characteristics of which were *socially* the complete insignificance of caste and property, *dogmatically* thorough atheism and deification of humanity, *morally* the dogma of the vanity and unreality of all earthly good, transmigration of the soul in accordance with the laws of moral retribution, and final absorption in Nirvâna.

But in spite of his undoubted originality of genius, it is more than probable, that he was not the *first* Buddhist, that he was but a great *reformer*, the

Martin Luther of a sect which existed perhaps for centuries before him, but which rose with *him* only into historical significance, and which *he* inspired with the courage to publicly compete with the national religion of the Brahmans and the various sects attached to the latter.

One other characteristic, imprinted upon Buddhism by his master hand, is the spirit of thorough liberality and absolute tolerance, which has marked the early rise and progress of Buddhism and which enabled it to adopt the most valuable ideas of all religions it came in contact with, to enter into a compromise with almost every form of popular superstition and to found and maintain a church, for thousand of years, without ever persecuting a single dissenter. That Buddhism is to the present day a system of unlimited eclecticism, is no doubt the work of the clever reformer Shâkyamuni Buddha himself.

This is well nigh all concerning the origin of Buddhism, that may be said to belong to history. But now let us see what Buddhist *tradition* reports on this same first epoch in the life of early Buddhism.

If we had the faith of an orthodox Buddhist, we should say, that the history of Buddhism is, like the history of the world, without a beginning. As from eternity one world has succeeded the other, rising into existence by a law of evolution, flourishing and perishing again, only to be substituted by another,—thus, in all these countless numbers of worlds, which have risen into existence and disappeared again, before our present world came into being, there have been Buddhas. And the religion of each of these former

Buddhas was subject to the same laws of rise, progress and decay.

Now in our present world, there have appeared already seven great Buddhas, the last and greatest of whom was, however, Shâkyamuni Gâutama Buddha. But before Shâkyamuni was born a *Buddha*, he had appeared on this earth at least 550 times, descending perhaps first in a flash of lightning, then may be vegetating as a humble plant, reborn again as a worm, again perhaps reborn as a snake, then as a beast, a bird and so forth. Thus in 550 successive stages of transmigration he worked his way up from the lowest forms of existence to the highest, through the various kingdoms of nature, through the different classes of sentient beings, then among the human race from the lowest caste to the highest and through all the various degrees of intellectual and religious saintship, exhibiting all the time, in every particular walk of life in which he appeared, the utmost unselfishness, absolutely self-denying and self-forgetting love and charity, constantly sacrificing his life for the benefit of other creatures animate and inanimate.

At last he was reborn in a certain heaven whence all Buddhas come down to earth. Knowing that he was now to be reborn on earth as a Buddha, he goes with the assistance of some other dévas through the whole court almanac of Indian princes and princesses, and finally selects the King of Kapilavastu and his young bride for his parents. In accordance with this choice, this virgin bride, whose name, Mâyâ, bears a curious resemblance to that of the mother of our Saviour, gives birth to a son, whilst a host of heavenly beings hasten to the spot and flashes of light announce to all the universe the birth of a Buddha: peace on earth and good will toward men.

The newborn babe is forthwith baptized, and an old saint, called Asita, appears like the Simeon of the gospel, takes him in his arms and with tears in his eyes he predicts the child's future destinies. He does so, however, by a phrenological examination of the baby's skull, on the top of which he remarks a curious bump, the indisputable indication of future Buddhaship. In further confirmation of his assertions he points out altogether 80 remarkable features of beauty, and especially a complete network of delicate tracery on the child's skin, where he observes a series of 32 ornamental symbolic designs most conspicuous on the palms and soles of the baby. In fact this wonderful child must have come into the world tattooed like a North American Indian.

A few years afterwards the baby was presented in a temple, when—lo and behold—all the statues and idols there rise and prostrate themselves before him. When seven years old, teachers are engaged for him, but the teachers find to their astonishment, that he knows more than they could teach him and retire dumb-founded. As gymnastic exercises seem then to have formed part of an Indian school education, he was taught gymnastics and excelled all competitors by strength of muscle. He threw a large elephant to a considerable distance, and shot an arrow so deep into the solid ground, that it laid bare a fountain of water.

But he, the most beautiful, the most learned, the most powerful of men, came to sad grief through women. He got married, and all Buddhistic traditions agree in stating, that it was the experiences he made with the ladies of his harem which disgusted him with the whole world and put him into such a misanthropical mood, that when he once, on a solitary walk, met with a miserable decrepid old man, a young man writhing in the agonies of disease, a dead corpse and—by way of striking contrast—a jolly-looking friar, he suddenly ran away from house and home and fled into the wilderness, and became a friar too.

In vain he endeavoured to regain his peace of mind by solitude, fasting and self-torturing asceticism. He tried all the prescriptions of Brahminism and Shivaism,—all in vain. When he was reduced by fasting and hunger to the last stage of exhaustion, Satan himself appeared to tempt him in various ways to a career of ambition and self-glorification and finally to a life of sensual pleasure; but by keeping his mind fixed on the idea of the utter unreality of all earthly things he conquers all such temptations.

Steeped in a sort of ecstatic meditation he remains seated under a tree a whole night, when at last he reaches the goal of absolute intelligence: he recognizes clearly that misery is a necessary attribute of sentient existence, that the accumulation of misery is caused by the passions, that the extinction of passion is possible through fixed meditation, and finally that the path to this extreme meditation results in the absorption of existence which would be a state of unlimited happiness. With the attaining of this fourfold truth he has freed himself from the bondage of sense, perception and self, he has broken with the material world, he lives in eternity; in one word: he has become a Buddha.

Forthwith he leaves the wilderness, when some "wise men from the East" appear and make him some offerings. He collects some disciples and begins —what must have been a perfectly novel thing in his time—a course of public open-air preaching. He wanders about from place to place, preaches in season and out of season, proclaiming everywhere that all earthly things are vanity and vexation of spirit.

By the irresistible force of his soul-stirring eloquence he gradually founds a new sect, a new religion. For everywhere crowds of fanatic followers gather round him, men of all ranks and all classes; all take the vow of perpetual chastity and voluntary poverty; all follow him about, clad in rags, begging and preaching.

Women also flock to him, but for a long time he refuses to admit them to the vows, for he is no advocate of women's rights and laid down the doctrine, which has ever since been retained by Buddhism, that a woman's highest aspiration should be to be reborn as a man. One of his favourite disciples, who is to the present day adored as the principal patron of female devotees, persuaded him however, to found an order of sisters of charity, thus giving women at least a chance of salvation. In this way the foundation was laid for an ecclesiastical organization, built up on the idea, that man and woman must, in order to be saved, become first priests and nuns. *Extra ecclesiam nulla salus.*

Buddha is said to have wandered through the length and breadth of India and through Ceylon, preaching everywhere the doctrine of universal misery and employing the terrors of transmigration and hell, to induce rich and poor to lay aside all other pursuits, and to devote themselves exclusively to the salvation of their souls, to religious meditation, to enter the church, to become priests and nuns.

To give weight to his authority he also worked miracles. But his miracles (as afterwards those of his disciples) were more like tricks of jugglery. He did not heal the sick, he did not recal the dead to life, but he showed himself suddenly sitting cross-legged in mid-air, divided his body into many portions, each shedding forth luminous rays, or he transported himself through the air hither and thither, to show that purely spiritual meditation can break through all the chains of material laws, that the spirit is independent of matter.

On the other hand, he, the son of a king, associated daily with the lowest and the outcast, went about in rags, begging his food from door to door and proclaiming everywhere in the face of that powerful caste-spirit of India that his religion was a religion of mercy for *all*. As a teacher he displayed great liberality and tolerance, adopting for instance all those deities which were decidedly popular, though he inded assigned them a signally inferior position in his system, for the holy man, he used to say, is above the gods.

Those Brahmanic and Shivaitic sects however, which were plainly immoral, he attacked and fought against with all weapons at his command, conquering generally more through superiority of magic power, than through logical argumentations.

He remodelled almost every Brahmanic dogma, so far as it was necessary, in order to destroy its pantheistic aharacter, for which he substituted his down-right atheism. But it is significant that he placed every Brahmanic doctrine into a new light by the preponderance of *ethical* treatment, which characterized his teaching to the almost total exclusion of pure metaphysics.

In this way he laboured for a series of years. But not satisfied with spreading his religion on earth he is also said to have ascended up into the heavens and to have gone down to hell, to preach everywhere the way of salvation.

Towards the end of his life he is said to have been glorified, or, as the Buddhist tradition literally calls it, baptized with fire. He was on a mountain in Ceylon, discoursing on religious subjects, when suddenly a flame of light descended upon him, and encircled the crown of his head with a halo of light.

When he felt his end drawing near, he turned his way to Kushinagara, N.W. of Patna. Heaven and earth began to tremble and loud voices were heard, all living beings groaning together and bewailing his departure. On passing through Kushinagara a poor workman offered him his last meal, and though he had just refused the offerings of the highest and richest, he accepted this offer, to show his humility, as he said, "for the sake of humanity." Immediately afterwards he said to his disciples "stand up, let us go, my time is come." He went out to a spot, where eight trees in groups of two were planted together. Resting on his right side he gave his final instructions to his disciples, reminded them of the immortality of the spiritual body and then gave himself up to contemplation.

Passing through the various degrees of meditation which correspond to the various tiers of heaven, he lost himself into Nirvâna and thus his earthly career was ended. His disciples put his remains into a golden coffin which immediately grew so heavy, that no power could move it. But suddenly his long deceased mother Mâyâ appeared from above, bewailing her son, when the coffin lifted itself up, the lid sprang open, and Shâkyamuni appeared with folded hands, saluting his mother.

Afterwards, when his disciples wanted to perform the ceremony of cremation, they discovered that his body was incombustible by ordinary fire, but suddenly a jet of flame burst out of the mystic character inscribed on Buddha's breast and reduced his body to ashes. The latter were eagerly collected and received thenceforth almost divine worship, being carried to all Buddhist countries, and for safe keeping deposited in pagodas expressly built for this purpose.

Attentive readers will have noticed in this rough sketch of Buddha's life many details coinciding with incidents of the life of our Saviour as reported by the gospels.

Shâkyamuni Buddha—we are told—came from heaven, was born of a virgin, welcomed by angels, received by an old saint who was endowed with prophetic vision, presented in a temple, baptized with water and afterwards baptized with fire, he astonished the most learned doctors "by his understanding and answers," he was led by the spirit into the wilderness, and having been tempted by the devil, he went about preaching and doing wonders. The friend of publicans and sinners, he is transfigured on a mount, descends to hell, ascends up to heaven,—in short, with the single exception of Christ's crucifixion, almost every characteristic incident in Christ's life is also to be found narrated in the Buddhistic traditions of the life of Shâkyamuni Gâutama Buddha.

And yet, this Buddha lived and died 543 years before Christ! Are we to conclude then, that Christ —as a certain sceptic would make us believe—went to India, during the 18 years which intervened between his youth and manhood, and returned, 30 years old, to ape and reproduce the life and doings of Shâkyamuni Buddha? Or are we, who believe in Christ's originality, driven to the miserable subterfuge of assuming—as some Jesuit fathers do—that the devil, foreknowing the several details of the promised Messiah's life, anticipated him and all the details of his life by his own caricature in Shâkyamuni Buddha?

Unfortunately for the sceptic who would delight in proving Christ to have been the ape of Buddha, it can be proved, that almost every single tint of this Christian colouring, which Buddhist tradition gives to the life of Buddha, is of comparatively modern origin. There is not a single Buddhist manuscript in existence which could vie, in antiquity and undoubted authenticity, with the oldest codices of the gospels. Besides, the most ancient Buddhistic classics contain scarcely any details of Buddha's life, and none whatever of those above mentioned peculiarly Christian characteristics. Nearly all the above given legends, which claim to refer to events that happened many centuries before Christ, cannot be proved to have been in circulation earlier than the fifth or sixth centuries *after* Christ. Moreover I shall presently have an opportunity to point out the precise source from which those apparently Christian elements flowed into and mingled with Buddhistic traditions concerning the life of Buddha.

I have entered thus fully into the detailed history of the founder of Buddhism, because it is, in my opinion, an indispensable key to the understanding of Buddhism as a whole, for every single Buddhist dogma is believed to have been evolved from the intuitive consciousness or inward experience of this one man. To the present day, any dogma, even of the latest growth, will be received by the most orthodox Buddhist, if it can be made to fit into the inner history of the great Shâkyamuni Buddha, as reported by tradition.

After his death a general assembly of the faithful was called, and the legends assert that then and there the sayings and teachings of Buddha were collected, sifted and fixed in a triple canon, by the three principal disciples of Shâkyamuni. But for centuries after, we have no proof whatever of the existence of a written canon.

On the contrary, the doctrines of Buddha appear to have been handed down from generation to generation orally. One of Buddha's disciples distinguished himself above his fellows and was soon looked upon as the successor of Shâkyamuni. He appointed his successor, handing over to him his almsbowl and his mantle, together with some pithy sayings, embodying the essence and substance of Buddhist doctrine. This one again appointed his successor in the same way, and thus we have a series of patriarchs, as they were called, who in turn were looked upon each as the temporary head of the church of his time, and who transmitted from generation to generation the reputed teaching of Shâkyamuni Buddha.

Of course the Buddhist dogma underwent considerable alterations in thus passing from mouth to mouth. Naturally also heresics sprang up here and there, for the putting down of which again and again œcumenic councils were held, to re-establish the orthodox doctrines in opposition to heretical adulterations.

About the beginning of the Christian era many books also seem to have been in circulation, claiming to be authentic expositions of the orthodox faith. A number of them would appear to have received public approval at the œcumenic council, held in Cashmere under Kanichka, who reigned from 15 B.C. to 45 A.D., and to have been gathered in three divisions to form the standard canon of the Buddhist Church.

But no reliable information exists as to the extent and character of the Buddhist scriptures said to have been finally revised by that council. The very earliest compilation of the modern Buddhist canon, that *history* can point out, is that of Ceylon. But the canon of Ceylon was handed down orally from generation to generation. Part of it was reduced to writing about 93 B.C. [under the reign of Wattagamini, 104-76 B.C.]. The whole canon, however, was first compiled and fixed in writing between the years 412 and 432 of our present Christian era.

Burmese and Siamese Buddhists received their sacred scriptures from Ceylon. But the canon of Northern Buddhists, that is to say that of Cashmere, Nepaul, Tibet, Mongolia, China, Corea and Japan, this Northern canon, which claims to have been formed earlier, by the above-mentioned fourth council, coincides with the Buddhist scriptures of Ceylon, though the Northern Buddhists have apparently enlarged the original canon to a great extent.

So much about the bible of the Buddhist Church. As to this church itself, it was left at the death of Shâkyamuni Buddha with the mere rudiments of an ecclesiastical organization. But his followers enthusiastically and consistently went on completing the edifice. They continued to preach and to teach much in the same way as Shâkyamuni himself had done.

Soon, however, they found it necessary to moderate their demands. It was for instance practically impossible that every one should become a priest. Thus lay-brethren and lay-sisters were admitted into the church with a relaxation of the vows. Then in the various monasteries and nunneries, which sprang up everywhere, discipline had to be maintained, different occupations and different age produced a difference of rank, and thus slowly but steadily a complete machinery of ecclesiastical and monastic organization was formed, with an elaborate code-book of discipline and ceremonial.

Whilst the Buddhist church was thus internally occupied, consolidating itself and gaining in stability and strength, it could not be expected to spread to any great distance, especially as India was then politically divided into innumerable petty kingdoms, in most of which the Brahmans exercised paramount influence.

Consequently we find, that during the first two centuries after the death of Buddha, from 543 to 325 B.C., the influence of the new religion was confined to the countries bordering on the Ganges and had scarcely reached the Punjab.

At the end of this period Alexander the Great invaded India. But strange to say, of this glorious campaign of the Greek armies, which for the first time brought India into close contact with Hellenic civilisation and culture, no traces remain, except on the part of India a few coins and inscriptions, and on the part of the Greeks a few mysterious legends, as for instance that of the Indian Hercules and a few scanty notes as to the existence of Buddhists in India.

But out of the political anarchy into which the whole conglomeration of Indian Kingdoms was thrown by the invasion of Alexander, arose an empire which soon swallowed up all the others.

It was founded by an adventurer of low birth called Tchandragupta by the Buddhists, and Sandracottos by the Greek historians. Despised on account of his low birth by the Brahmans, he hated them in return and began to patronize the rising Buddhist church. His grandson Ashôka, whose cognomen Piyadasi has been handed down to the present day by innumerable stone inscriptions scattered all over India, united nearly the whole of India under his sceptre. Embracing the Buddhist faith, in which he saw the safeguard of his dynasty, he strengthened and extended the Buddhist church with all the means at his command, and became the Constantine of Indian Buddhism.

Ashôka formally acknowledged to hold his power and possessions only as a fief from the church, he convoked an œcumenic council for the establishing of orthodox teaching, tightened the reigns of church discipline by the introduction of quinquennial assemblies to be held in each diocese, erected pagodas and endowed monasteries with great profusion in all parts of India.

But the greatest work he did was the establishing of a board for foreign Missions (Dharma-Mahamâtra), which sent forth to all surrounding countries enthusiastic preachers who went out in self-chosen poverty, clad in rags, with the almsbowl in their hands, but supported by the whole weight of Ashôka's political and diplomatic influence. His own son Mahêndra went out as a missionary to Ceylon, and the whole island forthwith embraced the faith of Buddha.

At the same time Cabulistan, Gandhara, Cashmere and Nepaul were brought under the influence of Buddhism, and thenceforth every caravan of traders, that left India for Central Asia, was accompanied by Buddhist missionaries.

In this way it happened, that as early as 250 B.C. a number of 18 Buddhistic emissaries reached China, where they are held in remembrance to the present day, their images occupying a conspicuous place in every larger temple.

So then we observe with regard to these earliest Buddhist missionaries three things which may perhaps contain a hint fo the solution of the modern question of missionary difficulties in China. These Buddhist missionaries went out, in the first instance, with even greater self-abnegation than Roman Catholic priests, as mendicant monks; secondly, they followed in the wake of trade; and thirdly, they were backed by the "inevitable gunboat" of imperial influence and diplomacy.

But soon after Ashôka's death his empire fell to pieces, the Brahmans lifted their heads up again, and a reaction took place which resulted in a severe persecution of all Buddhists then living in India.

In the course of this dark period, which reached its height under Pushpamitra in 178 B.C., most of the monasteries and pagodas were laid in ashes, nearly all the sacred books were destroyed, and the whole Buddhist church in India received a shock from which it never afterwards recovered. But this very persecution gave a renewed impetus to the foreign missions of the Buddhists, who now pushed their way through the whole of Central Asia and gained a lasting foothold among the various Tartar tribes which were just then in great commotion.

A branch of the great tribe of the Huns, pushed to the West by the advances of the Chinese in Central Asia, fell over the Greek provinces West of the Hindukush, overran Trans-oxania, destroyed the Bactrian kingdom and finally conquered the Punjab, Cashmere and the greater part of India.

Their greatest king Kanishka, a contemporary of Christ, patronized Buddhism as liberally as Ashôka had done. During his reign the last œcumenical council, which revised the canon, was held in Cashmere, but it was not recognized by the Buddhist church of Ceylon, and thus a split took place, corresponding to the division of the Roman and Greek churches in the ecclesiastical history of the West.

The Buddhist church of Ceylon, with its dependencies in Burmah and Siam, maintained with great tenacity the original teaching of early Buddhism in comparative purity, whilst the Northern Buddhists, that is to say those of Northern India, Cashmere, Nepaul and afterwards those of China, Tibet and Mongolia, went on constantly adding to and expanding the common stock of doctrines and traditions, and entering into compromises with any form of popular superstition they found too deep-rooted and too popular to overcome.

About this time it was that Buddhism was officially recognized in China. I have remarked above, that as early as 250 B.C. Buddhist missionaries peregrinated through China. They found there a popular religion, the chief characteristics of which were serpent and tree-worship, the grand moral system of Confucianism and the system of Tauism, which had already descended from its sublime height of philosophic mysticism to an alliance with popular forms of superstition, sorcery and witchcraft. The Buddhists at once arrayed themselves on the side of popular superstition and Tauism, in opposition to Confucianism. But for fully 300 years, from 250 B.C. to 62 A.D. the labours of Buddhists in China met with little success; in fact, statistic enquirers into the missionary problem would have called it a decided failure.

Meanwhile, however, Chinese armies had been fighting a series of campaigns in Central Asia and had repeatedly come into contact with Buddhism established there. Repeatedly it happened that Chinese generals, engaged in that war, had occasion to refer in their reports to the throne to the influence of Buddhism, and in the second year before Christ an ambassador of the Tochari Tartars (probably sent by Kanishka) presented the emperor of China with a number of the sacred books of Buddhism.

More than a hundred years before that time, in the year 121 B.C., a gigantic golden statue of Buddha forming part of the spoils of those campaigns had been brought to the Chinese court.

If we keep these facts in mind, there is no apparent reason why we should discredit the story of the famous dream of the Emperor Ming-ti. It is reported in Chinese history, that in the year 61 A.D. the Emperor Ming-ti saw in a vision of the night an image of gigantic dimensions, resplendent as gold, its head surrounded by a halo as bright as the sun, approach his palace and enter it. At a loss how to explain this dream, the Emperor appealed to his younger brother, the prince of Thsu, who had been known for years as the most zealous protector of the Tauists and who probably favoured Buddhism too. At any rate, this prince at once suggested, that the golden image which the Emperor saw referred to the statue of Buddha, and that it seemed to be Heaven's command, that Buddhism should be introduced at court and adopted by the Imperial Government.

Thereupon the Emperor despatched an embassy, which passed through Central Asia, to Cashmere and India, and returned in 75 A.D. accompanied by a Hindoo priest, with a statue of Buddha, carved in sandalwood, and one sacred book. The latter was forthwith translated and published by Imperial authority, and therewith Buddhism was firmly established in China.

Soon other Hindoos arrived in China with more books, which were likewise translated by order of succeeding Emperors. In fact, Chinese Buddhists appear to have been most anxious to obtain and translate as many Buddhist manuscripts as they could lay hold of. Several Chinese Emperors interested themselves in this work. And yet, more than 300 years after Ming-ti had sent his embassy to India to collect the sacred books of Buddhism, the emperor Yau-Ling in 397–415 A.D. had to send an expedition to Central Asia, to obtain more books, and about the same time the famous traveller. Fahien started for India on account of the absence of books treating on ecclesiastical discipline. Again in 518 A.D. the Queen of the Wei country sent ambassadors to India for Buddhistic books, and in 629 the celebrated Hiuen-tsang set out on his travels through Central Asia and India, with the same object in view.

In 860 A.D. the Emperor I-tsung of the Tang dynasty applied himself to the study of Sanskrit and gave a new impetus to the collection of Buddhistic literature, which was now only approaching completion. The Emperor Jin-tsung opened a college for Sanskrit studies in 1035 A.D. and appointed fifty youths to study that language.

And yet, in spite of all these strenuous efforts, continued for more than a thousand years, it was not until the year 1410 A.D. that the Chinese procured a complete edition of the Buddhist canon, and the modern edition of it, known as the Northern collection, is of still later date, having been completed between the years 1573-1619 A.D.

What becomes then of the assertion that the Buddhist canon was closed at the time of the fourth œcumenic council under Kanishka? Kanishka died in 45 A.D. Scarcely 25 years afterwards Ming-ti's embassy arrived in the very place, where that council had been assembled, and having searched all through India for Buddhistic books returned to China with a tiny little volume.

It is clear therefore that history bears me out in what I said above that the earliest edition of the Buddhist scriptures is that of Ceylon, which according to the unanimous testimony of Singhalese Buddhists did not exist before the years 410-432 A.D. Next comes the Chinese canon collected under the Tang dynasty (about 860 A.D.) and completed in 1410 A.D.

We see therefore how favourably our Christian Bible compares with the canon of the Buddhists. Our Bible has been assailed by sceptics and infidels, has been historically and critically examined under the microscope of prejudiced antiquarians, and yet the fact remains uncontested that the canon of the Old Testament was completed in Esra's time about 450 B.C. and that no farther additions were made to the canonical books of the New Testament after the close of the second century of our era. Besides, we still possess ancient manuscripts of the New Testament, one of which, the Codex Vaticanus, was written in the course of the fourth century, one hundred years before the first edition of the Buddhist scriptures was undertaken, of which not a single ancient manuscript has withstood the ravages of time, and which has never yet been examined critically by either friend or foe.

But to return to our subject, we have seen that Buddhism split about the beginning of the Christian era into two divisions, which are now-a-days known under the names of Southern and Northern Buddhism.

Southern Buddhism, *i.e.*, the Buddhists of India, Ceylon, Burmah and Siam, soon lost considerable ground. New persecutions broke out again and again at the instigation of the Brahmans, especially in India, where the last remnants of Buddhism were exposed to the most sanguinary persecution in the course of the sixth and seventh centuries. But no detailed records of this struggle remain. Certain however is it that these persecutions, followed up by the invasion of the Mahomedans, put an end to the reign of Buddhism in India, and at the present day there are in India but scanty traces of its former existence, in the shape of ruins, rock temples and the sect of Djains, whose connection with Buddhism is now scarcely recognizable.

In Ceylon, in Burmah and Siam, Buddhism is still flourishing. Its doctrines are popularly believed in, and practically obeyed, though the priests themselves are generally despised, unless they are objects of awe on account of supposed magic powers. The temples and monasteries are in possession of large revenues, and yet the sacred buildings are everywhere allowed to fall into ruins, scarcely an effort being made to prevent their destruction by the elements of nature. The number of priests now living in Ceylon does not average more than one in 400 of the whole population. This would give for the island about 2,500 priests. The proportion is much less than in Burmah, where again priests are fewer than in Siam, though the temples are more numerous.

But whilst Southern Buddhism lost the greater part of its ancient territory, Northern Buddhism has since the beginning of our Christian era run a course of almost unchecked conquests.

It retained its foothold in Cashmere and Nepaul, and though it lost most of its influence in the Western half of Central Asia, through the influx of

Mahomedanism, it conquered new territories, vastly superior in extent and importance.

We have seen how it spread to China, where it was officially adopted in the year 61 A.D., and though the Confucianists in successive centuries persecuted Buddhism with fire and sword and put forth their best literary efforts to nullify its influence, they not only failed to stop the progress of Buddhism, but got themselves so imbued with Buddhistic ideas, and so impressed with its pretences of magic power, that to the present day the most thorough-paced Confucianist goes without any scruple through Buddhistic ceremonies, on the occasion of weddings or funerals, or in cases of illness, epidemic or drought. It was only the other day, that a Chinese gentleman, a Confucianist to the backbone, expressed in a conversation with me his utmost contempt for Buddhism, but at the same time, when I happened to show him a certain Buddhistic Sutra, he acknowledged to have learned it by heart. When I asked him how he came to study a Buddhistic book, he assured me with the greatest seriousness that it was universally known, and proved by his own experience, that the reading of this volume was a never-failing panacea for stomach-ache.

It is certainly wrong to say, that the Chinese are all Buddhists. The priests are not very numerous in China; they are recruited from the lowest classes, generally the most wretched specimens of humanity, more devoted to opium smoking than any other class in China. They have no intellectual tastes, they have ages ago ceased to cultivate the study of

Sanskrit, they know next to nothing about the history of their own religion, living together in idleness and occasionally going out to earn some money by reading litanies for the dead or acting as exorcists and sorcerers or quack doctors. No community of interest, no ties of social life, no object of generous ambition, beyond the satisfying of those wants which bind them to the cloister, diversify the monotonous current of their daily life.

And yet the whole of the Chinese people is influenced to a certain extent by the doctrines of Buddhism. Tauism is but Buddhism in native dress. The doctrines of transmigration, of hell and a future paradise in heaven, have penetrated far and wide among the mass of the people.

Where then is the much-talked-of exclusiveness of China? Buddhism is a foreign religion, introduced by foreign priests, of whom there were at the beginning of the sixth century upwards of 3,000 living in China. To the present day two-thirds of the whole Chinese Buddhistic literature are translations of foreign works. Every popular Buddhist book is full of Sanskrit phrases. The litanies which the priests read, the prayers which the common people recite, are Sanskrit!

Why then should we despair of bringing the Christian truth home to the hearts of this people? Christianity is more universal in its character and more adapted to the peculiarities of all nations than Buddhism. Christianity can be introduced in China without the study of a language as difficult as Sanskrit. The Chinese Christian Bible, as we already have it, is more intelligible to the common people, than any of the sacred books of the Buddhists. And truth must prevail in the end.

Let us remember, also, that it took Buddhism 300 years before it obtained official recognition, and many centuries more, before the mass of the people was influenced by it; and who will then speak of the failure of Protestant missions, which during the first 25 years of their operations in China gathered 5,000 natives under the banner of the gospel?

So much about China. From China Buddhism spread to Corea in 372 A.D. and thence to Japan, where it was first introduced in the year 552 A.D. But in both of these countries Buddhism has obtained but partial success, and suffered considerable adulteration by the influence of native religions.

The most complete triumph, however, that Buddhism ever achieved was accomplished in Tibet.

Buddhism was first introduced there during the reign of Lha-Lho-Lhori in 407 A.D., but it does not seem to have found many followers at first, and was already losing ground, though a great grandson of that king, called Srong-dsan-Gambo, favoured Buddhism and introduced Sanskrit studies and a Sanskrit alphabet in 629 A.D. But towards the end of the seventh century the inroads of the Mahomedans, putting an end to the Buddhist churches of Transoxania and Cabulistan, produced a new influx of Buddhist priests into Tibet.

King This-rong-de-tsan, who reigned 740–786 A.D., was the son of a Chinese princess and had inherited from his mother strong prejudices in favour of

Buddhism. During his minority the Tibetan nobles did their best to extinguish Buddhism. But the moment This-rong-de-tsan ascended the throne, all was reversed. Buddhism was officially adopted, learned priests were sent for from India, monasteries were built and endowed, and a beginning made with the translation of the Buddhist scriptures into Tibetan.

His successors also patronized the Buddhists and assisted them in the formation of a complete hierarchy, giving them spiritual jurisdiction, grants of land and various other privileges. This increase in church property and church influence, which of course enraged the nobility and impoverished the lower classes, produced a revolution, and a persecution broke out which endangered the very existence of Buddhism. But their persecutor King Lang-Darma having been assassinated by a priest, the persecution ceased.

Cautiously but speedily the Buddhists regained their former influence, and were soon stronger than ever, establishing an hereditary priesthood which thenceforth dominated over king and people.

This however led to general political anarchy, and to maintain his political influence, the spiritual metropolitan of Tibet found himself compelled to ask for the support of the Chinese Government, by means of which he and his successors, the so-called Grand Lamas, succeeded in appropriating to the church the political sovereignty over Tibet. High favour was manifested towards this influential body of ecclesiastics, who held in their hand the government of

Tibet, by the Mongol conquerors of China, and by means of their support it came to pass, that the heirs of the throne of Gengis Khan succeeded in reducing that kingdom to a feudal dependency of their own.

As to the inner history of the Tibetan church, Buddhism had there from the first entered into an alliance with the native religion, a form of Shamanism. Moreover, Buddhism was introduced into Tibet from Caferistan and Cashmere, where Shivaism and Brahmanism had been for a long time saturating Buddhism to the almost total oblivion of many of its original characteristics.

Thus it happened, that Buddhism reached Tibet in an adulterated form, and entering there into an amalgamation with Shamanism and especially with the necromantic superstitions which were indigenous in Tibet, departed still farther from the original form of Indian Buddhism. But when the study of Sanskrit was introduced in Tibet, and the canon collected and translated, a party arose which demanded a reform.

For a long time it struggled in vain. Meanwhile Nestorian missionaries had reached Central Asia, and some of that sect of reformers became acquainted with the story of Christ's life and the ceremonial of the Catholic church. True to the eclectic instinct of Buddhism they adopted many Christian ideas, traditions and ceremonies, and when their party afterwards obtained the mastery in Tibet, they reorganized the Tibetan church, amalgamating with it as many Christian forms as were compatible with Buddhistic orthodoxy.

Here we have then the explanation of the abovementioned coincidences in the traditions concerning the life of Buddha with the gospel narratives of Christ's life. And it is not a matter of surprise therefore, if we are told, that the Buddhist church of Tibet has its pope, cardinals, bishops, priests and nuns; that the Buddhists in Tibet have their infant baptism, their confirmation, their mass for the dead, rosaries, chaplets, candles and holy water, their processions, saints' days, fast days, and so forth. Many of these Christian ceremonies and traditions found their way into the Buddhist Church of China and its literature, though never to the extent practised in Tibet.

From Tibet Buddhism spread to Mongolia and Manchuria, where it prospered exceedingly. Every third person one meets in Mongolia is a priest, and many of their monasteries are as large as a good-sized town. To the Kalmyks on the Wolga, and the Burjuds on the Baikal sea, Buddhism has been carried at a comparatively recent period.

In conclusion, I will only say, that Buddhism, considered merely as an event in history, seems to me to have been more of a blessing than a curse.

I sincerely believe, that Buddhism has fulfilled a great mission which it was appointed to fulfil, by the providence of God. Nations, which were living in a state of utter savageness, were brought into a state of semi-civilisation, which is the more apparent, if we consider in what a savage state all those tribes remained which rejected Buddhism.

What the Mongols were before they became Buddhists, is written with blood on the pages of Asiatic history. Those very countries and peoples, which were shut out from the centres of civilisation by mountains and deserts, were visited and brought under the influence of morality by those indefatigable Buddhist zealots, for whom no mountain was too high, no desert too dreary. In countries like China and Japan, where Buddhism found a sort of civilisation existing, it acted like a dissolving acid, undermining the existing religious systems, and thus preparing the way for a new religion to enter,—for Christianity, if *we* had but half the enthusiasm that inspired those disciples of Buddha.

LECTURE THE SECOND.

BUDDHISM, A THEORETICAL SYSTEM.

In the preceding lecture on the subject of Buddhism I treated this grand system of religion merely as an event in history, and endeavoured to give to my readers an outline of its origin, rise and progress, combined with a brief sketch of its present condition and extent. If I have not altogether failed in my attempt to define the place which Buddhism occupies in the history of the world, and to assist the reader in forming a correct estimate of the manner in which it fulfilled its great mission to one third of the human race, he must have felt with me, that Buddhism is but "a voice that crieth in the wilderness."

The religion of Buddhism arose from a natural reaction and protest against the abnormal features, religious and social, of Brahmanism. It was fostered and sustained by the instinctive cry of the better part in human nature for release from the misery and hollowness of this present evil world; and thus it succeeded in spreading more or less throughout Eastern Asia a lively yearning for an invisible better world, for a paradise of peace and happiness beyond the range of mortal ken.

But it remains now to show what it was that voice proclaimed, what means it employed to rouse the dormant conscience, what food it offered to hungry and thirsty souls, what discipline it enforced to regulate man's conduct, what elements of truth it conveyed to the seekers of it. In one word, having viewed Buddhism as an event in history, I now proceed to consider Buddhism as a religious system, from a doctrinal point of view.

No religion on earth has ever remained stationary for any length of time. The Christianity of to-day is not and cannot be made to return to what it was eighteen hundred years ago. The Buddhist religion has undergone still more changes in the course of time, through the absence of a written canon at its first starting, through the influence of oral propagation and tradition, through contact with different religions and forms of superstition, and—last but not least—through the reaction of different nationalities which it more or less fully conquered.

Naturally therefore I feel tempted to again treat our subject historically. I might start with a sketch of the Buddhist dogma in its primitive form, as it first came out of the hands of him who gave to it the characteristics and general shape which no after revolution has been able to efface. It was then a system, diametrically opposed to Brahmanism whence it had arisen, and yet still possessing many marks of resemblance; a conglomeration of ideas, partly original, partly borrowed from Brahmanism and early Shivaism, but now clothed in the new garb of Buddhism, hastily thrown over and as yet as ill fitting as Saul's armour upon David.

I might then note the first attempt made to reduce the chaos of new and borrowed ideas into systematic order, the first phase of the development through which the Buddhist dogma passed. It is now known under the name of the Hinâyana system, or the school of the small conveyance, a name referring to the various means by which consecutive forms of Buddhism offered to "convey" the believer across the ocean of misery, to the shores of salvation, into the haven of Nirvâna.

This first period in the development of the Buddhist dogma is called the small conveyance, because the forms of doctrine and of worship were limited, plain, and simple then, compared with the elaborate systems of after times. Buddhism was then a system of exclusively moral asceticism, teaching certain commandments, rigorously enforcing an ascetic life of the strictest morality, temperance, and active, self-denying and self-sacrificing charity.

But soon after the beginning of our Christian era, when Buddhism had overcome its first difficulties and had leisure to enjoy the first taste of triumph, having spread from India to Ceylon, and northwards, through the Punjab, into Central Asia and across the Himalaya as far as China,—the energetic, practical asceticism of the Hinâyana school was replaced by a new phase of doctrine, called the Mahâyana system, or the school of the great conveyance. The characteristics of this system are an excess of transcendental speculation, which soon drifted into listless quietism or abstract nihilism, and substituted fanciful degrees of contemplation and ecstatic meditation for plain practical morality.

It was the former school, the system of the small conveyance, that produced the men who actually resigned their all, and with irresistible energy and enthusiasm spread Buddhism far and wide all over Eastern Asia—the men, who for their faith in Buddha scaled the snowy mountains of the Himalaya and crossed the sandy deserts of Central Asia. But now this Mahâyana system—this school of the great conveyance, with its refined philosophy and abstruse metaphysics, with its elaborate ritual and idolatrous symbolism—produced an entirely different type of heroes; men, who would glory in public disputations, who would let the most subtle dialectician come forth and split a hair,—they would split it over and over again; men, who would retire into the stillness of deserts or the solitude of mountain dens, or shut themselves up in the monotony of cloister life, to muse, brood and dream, like Tennyson's lotos-eaters; men, who like the first Chinese patriarch would sit twelve years gazing at a wall without moving, without speaking, without thinking.

The Hinâyana school however remained, though overpowered, yet still exerting some influence, and an attempt was made in the so-called Madhyimâyana school, or the system of the medium conveyance, to combine the above mentioned two schools, to find the golden mean between practical asceticism and quietistic transcendentalism, but—like all compromises

—it never gained much influence and found but few followers.

For a new system soon arose, more powerful, more fascinating than any of its predecessors. It is known by the name of the Tantra school. The hermits of the mountains had become acquainted with the medicinal properties of many herbs and professed to possess the elixir of immortality (which—I suspect —was but opium from India). The monks in the cloisters had become adepts in the black art, and became mantists, sorcerers and exorcists, who would banish drought, famine, pestilence, disease and devils by magic incantations. Thus practically useful, and fortified by alliance with the various forms of popular superstition, the Tantra school extracted moreover from the Mahâyana system all that was congenial with its own tendencies, and thus produced a new system of practical philosophic mysticism, sorcery and witchcraft, and overlaid the ritual of the Buddhist church with fantastic ceremonies and mystic liturgies.

It was this school that turned out the priests, who, as rain-makers, geomancers, or astrologers, duped emperors and peoples, and who exercise to the present day in the whole of Eastern Asia the strongest influence over the lower classes, as sorcerers, exorcists, physicians. They chant the litanies for the dead; they save souls from hell. But while the Tantra school thus gained the day with the multitude, through its practical usefulness and politic accommodation to the superstitious element in human nature, the Mahâyana school continued to exert a powerful influence in the province of literature, among the educated and the learned, and produced many different schools of philosophy, of which not less than eighteen are known by name.

Moreover the ancient Hinâyana school also retained its foothold to some extent, or was revived here and there, in different countries by certain sects. In fact, every one of the above-mentioned forms of development, through which the Buddhist dogma passed in the course of centuries, has left its deposit behind, in the form of sects, or schools, or parties, still existing in modern Buddhism. But these are not separated by prominent landmarks from each other, they run into and intermingle with each other, more or less, in almost every country.

Now under these circumstances it seems to me, that, at least for a popular lecture like this, an historical synthetic treatment of the rise, progress, and development of the Buddhist dogma would become an exceedingly complicated task, necessitating many reiterations, multifarious distinctions and limitations. And after all, if treated with the necessary minuteness and detailed accuracy, it would fail to produce a complete and at the same time intelligible picture. It would be more like a drama, not wanting indeed in progress of action, rich in striking incidents, difference of characters and varied beauty of pageantry, but too complicated to be perspicuous and too full of promiscuous details to bring home to the spectator the hidden unity of the whole.

I prefer therefore to adopt a different course. Instead of building up before the eyes of my readers the whole edifice of Buddhistic doctrines from the very foundations, instead of showing to them how one stone was laid upon the other, how one tier was raised upon the other, how one gallery intercommunicates with or crosses the other, I will give but a general sketch of the completed structure, a bird's-eye view of the whole.

For vast, intricate, and puzzling as the system of Buddhism appears to any one that enters its sacred halls, wanders from shrine to shrine, through its temples and cloisters, gazes at its pagodas and images, or searches through its libraries, rich in ancient and modern lore,—the whole labyrinth becomes plain and intelligible, when looked at from a distance, when one sees the very ground plan on which it has been constructed, when no bewildering details obstruct the view of the grand, simple and natural outlines of the whole.

For one plan, clear and distinct, underlies the whole network of Buddhistic doctrines. One continuous thread runs straight through the whole tangled woof of seeming dogmatic confusion. In spite of the changes which time, difference of nationalities, different schools and modes of thinking have wrought, there is still discernible a group of fundamental doctrines which remained through all ages, in all countries, the common property of all Buddhists. And these very doctrines will be found to contain the essence and substance of the whole system.

I propose therefore to treat my subject analytically. I will first of all take hold of those general characteristics, arrange them systematically, and examine them more or less minutely. Then I may go on to the disputed points, to the points of difference, and see how Buddhism varies in different countries. This latter subject will however be reserved for the third lecture.

But one remark more is necessary, before I can begin with this task. The materials for a systematic exposition of the Buddhist dogma, in an intelligible and scientific form, are not ready to hand, and especially do not easily fit into our way of expressing thoughts and connecting ideas.

Again, there is nowhere in Buddhistic literature a *Hutterus redivivus*, a short but complete compendium of the whole range of dogmas; there is no catechism that would give you the whole system in a condensed, popular and intelligible form. One has to search through all the mines of Buddhistic literature, hunt up a stone here and there, quarry it, dress it, before you can handle it with the finer tools of European logic and fit it into the systematic classifications of Western thought.

Asiatic diction loves to clothe naked truths in the gaudy glittering apparel of symbolic, typical and allegorical language. As Asiatic architecture is characterized by richness of decoration, thus the grand structure of Buddhist dogmatology is so encumbered and overlaid with fantastic ornament, most of its truths so disguised in the form of myths, fables, parables or symbols, that many mistake the outer form for the substance, the shell for the kernel, and the result is, that a very master thought of vast speculative depth becomes ridiculous nonsense in the hand of a superficial expositor.

I will give but one example. It is said, for instance, in all Buddhistic works treating on cosmogony, that every universe comes into existence in the following manner: out of the chaos of waters rises a lotos flower, out of this flower rises the universe unfolding successively its various spheres, heavenly and terrestrial. Now, this same idea one may see repeated in popular Buddhistic literature, illustrated by wood-cuts which represent the chaos of water, with a thousand flowers floating on it, each lotos flower supporting a whole universe. And European expositors of Buddhism, repeating this gross representation of a speculative truth, treat it as a piece of absurdity, fancying that it is the belief of Buddhists that every universe sprouts out of an actual lotos flower of gigantic dimensions! But in reality the whole is a mere simile, and the idea conveyed in this flowery language of Buddhism is of highly poetic and truly speculative import, amounting to this: that, as a lotos flower, growing out of a hidden germ beneath the water, rises up, slowly, mysteriously, until it suddenly appears above the surface and unfolds its bud, leaves and pistils, in marvellous richness of colour and chastest beauty of form; thus also, in the system of worlds, each single universe rises into being, growing up out of a germ, the first origin of which is veiled in mystery, and finally emerges out of the chaos, gradually unfolding itself, one kingdom of nature succeeding the other, all forming one compact whole, pervaded by one breath, but varied in beauty and form. Truly an idea, so far removed from nonsense, that it might be taken for an utterance of

Darwin himself. It reminds one, in fact, of that unpretending little poem of Tennyson's:

> Flower in the crannied wall,
> I pluck you out of the crannies;—
> Hold you here, root and all, in my hand,
> Little flower—but if I could understand
> What you are, root and all, and all in all,
> I should know what God and man is.

In the same way many other doctrines of Buddhism, handed down from antiquity in language borrowed from types in vegetable or animal life, in allegories or by the use of symbols and mystic emblems, have been misunderstood and superciliously classed among antiquated notions and infantile babblings.

But considering that Buddhism was started when humanity was in its infancy, and that Buddhism addressed itself to the primary work of educating savage tribes, it was not only natural, but educationally wise, when it chose a crude, imperfect, infantile mode of expressing its thoughts, when it spoke to those rude tribes of Asia, children as they were, in the language of children.

I do not deny that, in many cases, and especially in all references to cosmology, astronomy, geography, and all other branches of natural science, it is not only the form of expression, but the ideas themselves, which are childish. The Buddhist scriptures have not observed the wise reticence with regard to natural science by which our Christian Bible is marked. They abound therefore with statements of extreme absurdity. They tell us, for instance, with the utmost gravity and with the authority of inspiration, that in the centre of every universe there is a high mountain, the lofty peak of which supports the heavenly mansions, whilst at the roots of this same mountain, far beneath the earth, there are grouped the innumerable chambers of hell; they tell us that in the centre of the Himalaya mountains there is one large sea, from which all the large rivers of the world take their origin, the Hoangho, the Ganges, the Indus and the Oxus; they inform us that the sea water contains salt, because the dragon-god of the Ocean, whenever one of his temporary fits of rage comes over him, throws up with his gigantic tail volumes of water which inundate even the heavenly mansions above, and it is this water, which flowing back carries with it all the filth accumulated in the drains and sewers of heaven, and thus, we are told, the sea water gets its nasty taste.

I allude to these things, because I believe it would be unjust to pick out all the queer and childish sayings with which the Buddhist scriptures and especially popular Buddhistic books abound, and lead people to imagine that Buddhism is little better than a string of nonsense.

The Buddhists never cared to preserve their sacred scriptures in their original integrity. Unlike our bible, the Buddhist canon has undergone wholesale textual alterations; it has been edited and reedited a great many times, and every editor introduced into the text the favourite ideas of his time and his school.

As to the popular literature of Buddhism and its absurdities, we might as well collect those little pamphlets on dreams, on sorcery, on lucky aud unlucky days, on the lives and miracles of saints, which circulate among Roman Catholic peasants,—but would that give us a true picture of Roman Catholicism? Thus it is with Buddhism.

Those crude, childish and absurd notions concerning the universe and physical science do not constitute Buddhism. This great religion, imperfect and false as it is to a great extent, does not stand or fall with such absurdities. They are merely accidental, unimportant outworks, which may fall by the advance of knowledge, which may be rased to the ground by the progress of civilisation, and yet the Buddhist fortress may remain as strong, as impregnable, as before. A Buddhist may adopt all the results of modern science, he may become a follower of Newton, a disciple of Darwin, and yet remain a Buddhist.

The strong point of Buddhism lies in its morality, and this morality is equal to the non-christian morality of our civilised world. It is not civilisation therefore, but Christianity alone, that has a chance against Buddhism, because Christianity alone teaches a morality loftier, stronger, holier than that of Buddhism, because Christianity alone can touch, can convert the heart, for there—in the heart of the natural man—it is where the roots of Buddhism lie.

I remarked above, that there is a train of ideas which form the foundation of the whole system of Buddhism and have been retained through all ages and in all countries as the common property of all Buddhists. To place these fundamental doctrines before my readers in a connected systematic form I will begin with the Buddhist views of physical nature.

Before Buddhism arose, the thinking minds of India had been taught to look upon the visible universe "as one stupendous whole, whose body nature is and God the soul." But this God, or Brahma, was viewed only in a pantheistic sense, as an impersonal substance, as the one uncreated, self-existent, immutable entity, from which the whole universe emanated, which pervades all forms of existence as the principle of life pervades the body, and into which all will ultimately be re-absorbed.

Buddhism took a different view of the universe. Buddhism knows no creative prime agent, no supramundane or ante-mundane principle, no pre-existing spirit, no primitive matter. The very idea of existence has no room in the Buddhist system. For all and everything is in a constant flux, rising into existence, ebbing away again, perpetually changing and reproducing itself in an eternal circle, without beginning, without end.

But Buddhism does not say that our world is without beginning or without end. For the universe, in which we live, is but one of an endless number of world systems. Every one of these innumerable co-existing worlds has a beginning and comes to an end, but only to be reconstructed again, in order to be destroyed again in endless succession. What is eternal therefore and absolutely without beginning is not any individual world or universe, but the mere law of revolution, the mere idea of constant rotation through formation, destruction and re-construction.

To the question, how the very first universe was originally brought into existence, and whence that eternal law of ceaseless reproduction came, Buddhism honestly confesses to have no reply. When this very query was put before Buddha, he remained silent, and after some pressure explained, that none but a Buddha might comprehend this problem, that the solution of it was absolutely beyond the understanding of a finite mind.

This acknowledgment of the limits of religious thought, honest and praiseworthy as it is, reveals to us the weakness of this system of Atheism. It acknowledged a design in nature, it recognized immutable laws underlying the endless modifications of organic and inorganic life, and attained, even so long as two thousand years ago, to that grand "Darwinian" idea of a pre-existing spontaneous tendency to variation as the real prime agent of the origin of species, but—like Darwin and his school—it stopped short of pointing out Him, who originated the first commencement of that so-called spontaneous tendency, and who laid into nature the law which regulates the whole process of natural selection, God, the creator and sustainer of the universe.

Regarding the way in which each world system rises into being out of the germ of a previous universe, the Buddhist scriptures speak in a rather obscure phraseology. Out of the chaos, produced by the destruction of a former universe, rises a cloud which sends down fructifying rain. Thereupon numberless buds of new worlds sprout up like lotos flowers, floating on the water, each world developing first its sublimest heavenly portion and then its terrestrial parts. In the latter also the lower regions and forms of existence are developed out of the nobler ones, the lower classes of sentient beings out of the higher ones. The earth itself is formed out of a mould that resembles the honey distilled in the cup of the lotos. The whole surface of the earth is of a golden colour, emitting a delightful fragrance, whilst a liquid is exuded that forms the first ambrosian food of sentient beings.

This whole process of formation is supported by four winds, a moist wind, a dry wind, a strengthening wind, and a beautifying wind; also by five clouds or atmospheric influences, one that destroys all heat, one that saturates all with moisture, one that dries up all moisture, one that produces the minerals, and one that keeps the different worlds asunder and produces a chasm between heaven and earth. This is called the period (Kalpa) of formation.

Then comes the stationary period, a time of continued formation, at the opening of which in each world a sun and a moon rise out of the water, whereupon—in consequence of the coarser food of which sentient beings begin to partake—arises the difference of sex, before not existing; soon after, heroes distinguish themselves above their fellows, and next, with the distinction of the four castes, society is established, and monarchs arise, followed in due course by Buddhas.

This period of continued formation is succeeded by a time of gradual destruction through the elements of water, fire and wind, the work of destruction beginning in every universe at the lowest forms and reaching to the highest, leaving however a germ for future re-construction untouched.

The period of destruction is supplemented by a period of continued destruction, working on the same principles and resulting finally in a total chaos, called the period of emptiness, which in turn again is followed by periods of formation, continued formation, destruction, continued destruction, emptiness and so on in endless succession.

But in spite of these alternate destructions and renovations of every universe, each successive world is homogeneous in its constituent parts, having the same continents of the same size, the same divisions of mountains, river-systems, nationalities, countries and even cities though under different names. Again, every world in all the infinite systems of the cosmos is floating in empty space, each earth having nothing beneath it but the circumambient air, whilst the interior of each earth is incandescent.

The structure also of each earth is the same in every universe. Four continents lie around a gigantic central mountain, about which sun, moon, planets and stars revolve. But the four continents are separated from each other by the sea and from the central mountain (which in fact represents the axis of the world) by seven concentric circles of rocks, each separated from the other by an ocean, an idea suggested probably by the orbit of the seven planets.

Above that central mountain are ranged the various tiers of heavens, inhabited like our earth by sentient beings, called devas, who take a constant interest in the spread of the Buddhist religion on earth. These heavens are however very different from the Christian idea of a heavenly paradise, for they represent but different stages of moral and intellectual life, and though the inhabitants of these heavens enjoy comparatively greater happiness and length of life than any being on earth, they live in the flesh and are subject to the same evils that flesh is heir to, though in a minor degree, in proportion to their moral and intellectual advancement.

At the foot of that central mountain are ranged the various tiers of hell, and as the heavens increase in ascending gradation in purity and happiness of life, so these hells increase downwards in horror and duration of torture, the lowest hell being the worst gehenna. Strange to say, though the Buddhists know a devil, whom they call Mâra, and ascribe to him the power of assuming any shape he pleases, especially that of woman, in order to tempt men from the path of virtue, the abode of this Satan is not in hell, he rules in the air like the Christian or rather Anti-Christian "prince of the power of the air." The Buddhist hells are ruled by Yama, who himself is suffering torture here, being among the hosts of criminals but *primus inter pares.*

Now those heavens above and all the heavenly bodies, the hells below with their innumerable chambers, the earth and even the air that surrounds the earth, all these localities are peopled with sentient beings, divided indeed into different classes, but all form one community of living beings, all pervaded by the desire to live, all doomed to die. Neither the pains of hell nor the joys of heaven are endless. Everywhere there is death. And death is everywhere followed, so long as the desire of existence has not been overcome, by re-birth either into one of the hells or heavens, or on earth or in the air, in some form of sentient existence or other, the particular condition of each individual being determined by the accumulated merit or demerit of his or her previous existence.

There we have the doctrine of transmigration. It is not an invention of Buddhism, though it fits marvellously well into its conception of the universe with its rotation of formation and renovation. Long before Buddha arose, metempsychosis was taught by Brahmanism. In fact, the fountain source of this doctrine may be traced back to the oldest code book of Asiatic nations, to the Vêda itself, which plainly taught the immortality of the soul and accustomed the Hindoo mind to consider death as but a second birth, thus paving the way for the development which the dogma of metempsychosis soon after received by succeeding generations.

It was the system of Brahmanism that first promulgated in India the idea of transmigration. Of Brahmà it is said in the Upanishads and in the code of Manu, that the whole universe emanated from it, by evolution, not by creation. But as everything emanates from Brahma, so everything returns to it. Brahma is the alpha and omega, it is both the fountain from which the stream of life breaks forth and the ocean into which it hastens to lose itself.

Thus the human soul emanates from Brahma, descends to a contact with matter, defiles itself and has therefore to pass through all the different gradations of animate nature, from the lowest form of existence to the highest and noblest, before it is purified enough to be fit for a final return into the pure shoreless ocean of Brahma. All nature is animate to the Pantheist, and the circle of transmigration is therefore of immense width. The soul may after the dissolution of the body ascend to the moon, to be clothed in a watery form, and returning pass successively through ether, air, vapour, mist and cloud into rain, and thus find its way into a vegetating plant and thence through the medium of nourishment into an animal embryo.

Only those who have succeeded in destroying all selfish thoughts and feelings by means of mental abstraction, the saints only, will rest after death by being freed from all distinctions of form or name; they will be dissolved into Brahma, with which they commingle and in which they lose themselves like a river in the ocean. Those however, who during their life-time indulged in selfishness, lust and passions, will be subject to innumerable births according to their moral condition. Every breathing being will after death be reborn in accordance with the general tendency of its inner life. Those who were moved by noble instincts or motives will be reborn as men of a high caste. To those who were inflamed by low desires and passions a lower caste will be allotted in their next birth, whilst those who degraded their souls by beastly desires will be reborn as beasts, say as rats or pigs or tigers. Their souls may even descend to a still lower circle of transmigration and, in the way above mentioned, be finally reborn as plants, whence they will have to work their way up again through the class of beasts and the various classes of human society, until they at last reach the goal of Buddha by continued self-purification.

Such are the main outlines of this grand popular system. It starts with the idea handed down from primitive antiquity by the Vêda, that the soul is indestructible and immortal because it is of divine origin. It proceeds then to work out the general principle, that every soul must be materially what it is spiritually, that is to say, it must be clothed in a body the nature of which corresponds to the inmost bent of the mind; a beastly man must be reborn a beast, a godly man must be united with God. Dividing the empire of nature according to the different castes of Hindoo society, it lays down the rule that the soul as it gradually purifies itself from contact with matter may have to pass through some or all of the different classes of nature until it is finally united with the deity. For only in absolute union and absorption in the deity can be found peace, rest and happiness.

Buddha adopted this pantheistic dogma of metempsychosis, though not without remoulding and recasting it so as to fit into his own atheistic system.

Buddha first of all stripped this Brahmanic idea of the soul's transmigration of the metaphysical garb in which his contemporaries had received it through the Vedanta philosophy. In vain we search Buddhistic literature for a metaphysical treatment of this deeply interesting problem. In vain we search for a distinct notion of the origin of each individual soul, which the Vedanta philosophy placed in Brahma.

Buddha gave the dogma of the soul's transmigration an exclusively moral basis. In the place of Brahma, the fountain source and goal of Brahmanic metempsychosis, he substituted the idea of Karma, i.e. merit and demerit. Whilst the Brahman believed each human soul to originate in and to be part and parcel of Brahma, Buddha taught, that about the primitive origin of each human soul nothing further could be said but this: that each living soul, after the dissolution of its previous embodiment, comes again into being and is endowed with a new body, in accordance with its moral merit or demerit accumulated in a previous form of existence. In other words, each sentient being is the product of its own moral worth, each living soul is born out of the germ of its moral actions.

Again, the Brahmans looked upon the stream of transmigration as flowing on by its own innate force, each soul being driven on by its own tendency, gravitating towards its original source, Brahma. Consequently transmigration was but a natural process, ruled by the laws of nature. But Buddha remodelled this doctrine into a moral process guided by the will and ruled by the moral or immoral actions of each individual soul. Man, he said, is doomed to pilgrimage through the whole creation only as far he himself will have it. He is the maker of his own fate. Happiness and misery lie in his own hands. As his present condition has been determined by his previous appearance in human existence, so will his future position be dependent on his actions in his present life. Cruelty, covetousness, falsehood, lust, drunkenness and other vices will heap up a stock of demerit producing re-birth in one of the hells or at least in some wretched condition of life upon earth, according to the amount of demerit in store. The practice of the opposite virtues will insure re-birth in one of the heavens or in some desirable condition upon earth according to the store of accumulated merit. But all such rewards or punishments awarded during the pilgrimage of the soul through manifold repetitions of sentient existence will continue only for a limited period and are not eternal.

Transmigration therefore, and its bitterest sting, hell, with all its horrors of torture, is but chastisement not aimless punishment, is but intended to purify, to wean the soul from its cleaving to existence, to expiate the sinful guilty being, not to extinguish it.

Another difference observable between the Brahmanic and Buddhistic conceptions of the doctrine of metempsychosis is this, that Buddhism narrowed the circle of transmigration. Whilst according to the Upanishads the path of transmigration passes even through inanimate nature, through the mineral and vegetable kingdoms, Buddha limited it to the sphere of animal organic life. No doubt, he did so, because he looked upon transmigration altogether as a moral process.

Of course this dogma of the soul's pilgrimage through nature is a mighty weapon in the hands of an eloquent preacher. There is nothing so very frightful to us descendants of Western nations in the idea of transmigration. There may be rather something attractive in it for many. For life is to us the highest blessing and death we hate. Many would therefore submit to a thousand deaths if they were to live again a thousand times, and they would not care much how their lives might be, for life is precious to us in itself. But a different thing altogether it is with the sons of hot climates, with the lazy indolent Hindoo, with the sedentary Chinaman. To him life itself has no particular fascination. He counts death—if he may rest after that—a blessing. To suffer, to suffer even the fiercest tortures of hell, to suffer even for millions of years, is not half as frightful an idea to him as to be forced to act, to labour, to work for æons, being subject to death indeed, but with no welcome rest after death, being condemned to die, only to be immediately reborn again, perhaps as a hard worked animal or an unclean cur. This is it which makes the hearts of Oriental nations tremble with terror, and this is the weapon with which crafty Buddhistic priests subdued the stubborn hearts of Eastern Asia.

The clever founder of Buddhism, Shakyamuni himself, knew this well, and therefore he made this dogma of the soul's transmigration the very centre of his system, and daily he preached it, and daily his fanatic followers spread this doctrine farther and farther.

They did not handle it, however, as a tenet of speculative philosophy, they did not treat it as a sort of esoteric mystery, only to be revealed to the initiated, but directly appealing to man's moral conscience they proffered this doctrine to all as the only satisfactory explanation of the unequal distribution of rewards and punishments for good and evil in this present world. Thus practically dealing with the doctrine of metempsychosis they passed over in silence all purely metaphysical questions which Brahmanism had been so busy with.

The consequence of these tactics was, that Buddhism succeeded in bringing home this doctrine to every heart in all its practical bearings, so that at the present day every class of people in Buddhistic countries, educated and uneducated, young and old, man and woman, among half-civilized and among nomadical communities, think and speak and act in perfect accordance with this dogma. It is to them exactly what hell and damnation is to Christian peoples.

Naturally therefore the question arises, what escape is there from this dizzy round of birth and death, what ultimate goal is there beyond the circle of transmigration? The answer is, there is indeed an escape. The means of it lie in morality and meditation, and the haven of final deliverance is Nirvâna.

This answer, echoed with perfect unanimity by all Buddhistic schools, though they differ from each other as to the relative merits of morality and meditation and as to the nature of Nirvâna, makes it necessary for a complete sketch of the Buddhist dogma to discuss these further points, the system of morality, speculative philosophy and the doctrine of Nirvâna. I will do so as briefly as possible.

The Buddhist system of morality is based on the example of Buddha's life. Imitate Buddha, conform yourself as much as possible to this type of perfection, such is the supreme precept of the religion. Now Buddha distinguished himself first of all during his 550 previous births by self-forgetting, self-sacrificing charity. To get rid of self, therefore, is the primary condition of a holy life. He who is without desire, dead to himself, he alone truly lives. This may be considered the elementary principle of Buddhist morality.

But as Buddha in his last birth renounced not only his own self, but the world and all worldly good and pleasure, as he left society, retired into solitude, observed the strictest chastity and temperance, Buddhist morality makes correspondingly further demands upon the self-denial of its adherents. The first five commandments of the Buddhist religion run as follows: thou shalt not kill that which has life, thou shalt not steal, thou shalt not commit any unchaste act, thou shalt not lie, thou shalt not drink any intoxicating liquor.

Here we have no doubt the form and extent of the system of Buddhistic morality as it was originally promulgated. We observe that the starting point of this code of morality is the idea of absolute selfrenunciation. Human life appeared to Buddha as full of misery because of its being full of selfish desire, whence he inferred, that the path of deliverance lies in the entire renunciation of all selfish desire, in the complete exstirpation even of the desire of existence itself.

Here lies the moral strength of Buddhism. It is a religion of unselfishness. But here also lies the radical defect of Buddhism. For this idea of utter self-abnegation sprang in Buddha but from a lively conviction of the impermanency and unreality of the world of sense, not from that aspiration after communing with a being of perfectly unselfish goodness, which kindled the genius of Plato and forms the deep root of Christian morality.

Buddhist morality is a morality without a God and without a conscience. There appears in Buddhism an utter want of an active principle of goodness. Buddhist morality does not endeavour to produce in man a conviction of sin, it does not appeal to his own inner sense of moral goodness. Buddhism does not attempt to purify the affections, to govern desire, to control passion, to renovate the heart, to regenerate, to sanctify the whole being. Its virtue is essentially negative. It enjoins men to cease from doing evil, it demands the total extinction of all desire, of all passion, but stops short of urging men to do good and has no assistance to offer by way of strengthening humanity in its struggle with the powers of evil.

This very absence of an active principle of goodness, the denial of God and the disregard of the human conscience, gave to Buddhist morality that spirit of melancholy despair which it breathes. When Shâkyamuni became a Buddha through recognising that everything earthly is impermanent and unreal, that human existence is necessarily and inseparably welded with misery, he was simply in a state of moral and intellectual despair. He threw overboard all faith in God and moral consciousness; he abandoned all hope for the actual world which appeared to him radically and irremediably bad; he saw no way of escape but that of the extinction of existence itself. The greatest happiness, he said, is not to be born, the next greatest is for those who have been born to die soon.

It was however but a consistent development of Buddha's own ethical principles when his followers, feeling the want of a positive code of morality, constructed a moral system, the chief characteristics of which are comprehended in a formula that was ever after the rudimentary confession of faith of all Buddhist neophytes, the so-called formula of refuge: I take my refuge in Buddha, *i.e.* I will imitate him and all his doing; I take my refuge in Dharma, *i.e.* I accept all his ideas of the impermanency of all earthly things and the necessity of absolute self-renunciation; I take my refuge in Samgha, *i.e.* I renounce society, property, matrimonial and family life and see no salvation outside the pale of the church.

In short, Buddhist morality developed itself into a code of monasticism which condescendingly allowed or rather connived at the existence of lay-brethren and lay-sisters, but which held out hope of salvation to none but those who renounced the world and entered the church as mendicant priests and nuns.

This system produced the most elaborate rules for the guidance of the priesthood, regulating their dress, their diet, their occupation, and prescribing the very manner of standing up and sitting down with the most pains-taking and pedantic minuteness. It enjoined public confession of faults, which led to a complete code-book of casuistry. It produced a code of criminal law for the maintenance of discipline. It developed ecclesiastical rank, grades of saintship, an elaborate ritual, a complete religious calendar and so forth.

Now this system of morality viewed as a whole was not without its good effects. It was admirably adapted to the preservation of religious and moral life in times of immorality and political anarchy, and especially to the primary work of taming savage tribes whom it weaned from habits of cruelty, blood-thirstiness and bestiality, whose intemperate habits were successfully checked by enjoining complete abstinence, and who were taught to obey the law and to submit to the rules of morality, and thus prepared for civilisation.

Again, this system of monasticism, which offered a welcome to people of all classes and all nations, formed an excellent substitute for the narrow-minded exclusiveness of caste in India. In countries where Buddhism failed to extirpate caste, as for instance in Ceylon, this monastic and ecclesiastical system modified the pretensions of caste and counterbalanced its evils. In other countries, where warfare, despotism and feudal systems lacerated the peace of Asiatic peoples, producing even greater evils than caste in India ever did, there this Buddhist system of monasticism came in most suitably, teaching the equality of all nations and establishing a common brotherhood, a grand international league of morality, fraternity and abstinence.

On the other hand, every system of monasticism is morally bad and leads to cramp the intellect. I say it is morally to be condemned because the self-abnegation originally involved in giving up a worldly life is soon for consistency's sake supplemented by a life of selfish or cowardly seclusion. Monasticism is also detrimental to a healthy development of the intellectual faculties, as history and experience abundantly prove.

In the case of Buddhism I need only point to the fact, that it produced no literature worthy to be compared with even that of China, let alone that of European nations; that it never encouraged art or science; that it failed to comprehend the importance of any of the problems of political and social life, and that Buddhist priests are now-a-days generally noted for their ignorance and indolence. Moreover this grand system of Buddhist monachism inherited the inevitable tendency of every system of minutely regulated observances, to degenerate into an external formalism. When the first burst of enthusiasm has passed, the religion that overleaps all earthly piety soon collapses into a religion of forms, into a system of Phariseeism equally irrational and immoral. This has actually happened in the case of Buddhism.

But the best test for the value of any system of morality is the position it assigns to woman. Here Buddhist morality is found signally wanting. The system of Buddhism leaves woman where it found her 2,000 years ago. Instead of educating and elevating her, instead of breaking those chains of slavery in which women were held all over Asia, instead of giving woman a position in society worthy of her innate purity, Buddhism grudgingly allowed women a place in the hierarchy as nuns, but with the distinct understanding that there was no hope of salvation for them unless through being reborn as men.

This idea of re-birth brings us to the last and most important defect of Buddhist morality. The idea of transmigration pervades the whole system of Buddhist ethics like a deadly poison. For the theory of a man's destiny being determined by the stock of merits and demerits accumulated in previous forms of existence, constitutes Buddhism a system of fatalism; whilst the idea of improving one's future prospect by works of super-erogation, converts morality into a vast scheme of profit and loss.

Hence the Chinese Buddhist actually keeps a debtor and creditor account with himself of the acts of each day, and at the end of the year he winds it up. If the balance is in his favour, it is carried on to the account of the next year, but if against him, something extra must be done to make up the deficiency.

Thus it happens, that this grand moral system of Buddhism, starting with the idea of the entire renunciation of self, ends in that downright selfishness, which abhors crime, not because of its sinfulness, but because it is a personal injury, which sees no moral pollution in sin, but merely a calamity to be deprecated, or a misfortune to be shunned.

Morality however is not in itself sufficient to break through the circle of transmigration, to carry men across the ocean of misery, to save them from the evils of existence. The object of morality is to practically extinguish the passions, to root out desire. But the deepest root, the first cause of desire, lies in theoretical ignorance, misconception, delusion.

To eradicate this delusion, therefore, to remove this ignorance and misconception regarding the outer and inner world, would be the final means of deliverance, would rid the self of all the trammels of existence, would actually lift the individual practically and theoretically out of the circle of transmigration and land him on the shores of Nirvâna. In one word, whilst morality practically extinguishes the desire of existence, abstract meditation or speculative philosophy extinguishes existence itself.

Morality and philosophy therefore are indispensable to each other, whatever their relative importance may be. As Christianity requires both, good works and faith, thus also Buddhism bases the idea of salvation on a combination of the two factors, moral action and abstract thought or intelligence.

As Buddhist morality requires men to imitate the doings of Buddha, thus also Buddhist philosophy invites men to conform to and to follow up the very idea of Buddha, for the word Buddha means literally "one who knows," *i.e.* one who knows the unreality of all phenomena, which knowledge is looked upon as the result of abstract meditation. The way in which Buddha departed from this world, by the mental process of inwardly realising the total impermanency and nothingness of all earthly forms of existence, of overcoming not only the desire of existence, but destroying existence itself by a purely intellectual logical process—this is the object of Buddhist philosophy, this is the final path to Nirvâna.

Unfortunately however Buddha's followers differed from each other in no other detail of doctrine so much as in the manner in which they built up their systems of philosophy. They seemed to take a delight in contradicting each other, and the consequence was, that Buddhism split into a great number of different philosophical schools, each starting from the same circle of ideas, as given above, and each coming to pretty nearly the same result, to the idea of Nirvâna. Buddhism developed nominalistic and realistic schools, divided itself into schools of Idealism and Materialism, produced systems of Positivism and Nihilism. And there is very little they have in common with each other beyond the following propositions, which form the fundamental ideas of the philosophic systems of all shades and all ages in the sphere of Buddhist orthodoxy.

All start from the so-called four truths (Aryânisatyâni) or the idea that misery is a necessary attribute of sentient existence, that the accumulation of misery is caused by desire, that the extinction of desire is possible and that there is a path that leads to that extinction.

Another leading proposition, common to all schools is this, that individual existence (personality) is made up by the following five constituents (Skandhas), the organized body, sensation, perception, discrimination and consciousness.

Again, there is tolerable unanimity as to a certain concatenation of cause and effect, which is considered to form the real explanation of the riddle of existence. There are twelve links (Nidânas) in this endless chain of cause and effect. Existence, it is said, is caused by 1, ignorance or delusion; ignorance produced 2, action; from action arises 3, consciousness, thence 4, substantiality, thence 5, the six organs of perception (eye, ear, nose, tongue, body and mind); from the action of these organs arises 6, sensation, thence comes 7, perception; thence 8, desire or lust; from this desire springs 9, the cleaving to existence, which produces 10, individual existence; the latter finds its expression in 11, birth, but birth invariably produces 12, decrepitude and death, and death, though it breaks up the above-mentioned five constituents (Skandhas) of individual life, leaves behind the reproductive power, a germ as it were, which has to run the same round again through ignorance, action, consciousness and so forth.

Here we have then again, in philosophy also, the same circle, which we observed before in the system of the physical universe and—in the form of transmigration—in the moral order of the world.

We see therefore, how fitly Buddhism at the very outset adopted the emblem of a wheel in order to typify the leading characteristics of its faith: What the cross is to the Christian Church, emblematically pointing to the central truth of theoretical and practical Christianity, the same as regards fulness of significance is to the Buddhist his Dharma Tchakra, the so-called "wheel of doctrine." As the Christian speaks of preaching the cross, so the Buddhist speaks of "turning the wheel of doctrine." For the idea of ceaseless rotation running through the whole system, branch and root, has made of Buddhism altogether a system of wheels within wheels. *Ecce signum.*

I have been turning this wheel before the eyes of my readers, and it is time now to stop it by way of pointing out what the final escape from this weary dizzy round is, which Buddhism offers by means of mental abstraction. What is Nirvâna?

There has been much dispute in the learned world among Buddhists and among European scholars, whether Nirvâna means absolute annihilation or not. I would humbly suggest, that if the learned writers on the subject, instead of presuming Buddhism to have been one and the same thing everywhere, and in all ages, instead of overlooking that Buddhism is one thing as a scientific system and another as a popular practical religion, had taken into consideration that there are as many different Buddhistic denominations, schools and parties, as there are Christian sects, it would have saved much useless disputation.

The doctrine of Nirvâna, like all other Buddhist doctrines, has been differently handled in different ages, by different schools, writers and preachers. I have given much thought to the subject, and the conclusions I arrive at are these.

In the absence of ancient manuscripts and by reason of the repeated textual alterations which the Buddhist canon suffered before it was fixed in the form in which we now have it, it is practically impossible to determine what Shâkyamuni Buddha himself taught on the subject. He *may* have looked upon Nirvâna as a state of personal immortality of the spirit, exempt from the eddies of transmigration and revelling in the enjoyment of unlimited happiness through the annihilation of all desire. He *may* have viewed Nirvâna as a state of absolute annihilation of personality and individual existence. It is impossible to decide which of the two views he actually held. But I am inclined to think he most probably left the question undecided in his own mind.

After Buddha's death, his followers may likewise have left the problem untouched for some time. But the most ancient Sutras which we possess coincide with the popular literature of modern Buddhism, in describing Nirvâna as a state of exemption from birth and death, as a condition of peace and felicity, implyiug not only the continuation of consciousness and personality, but an active interest in the progress of religion on earth, which occasionally prompts individuals, after having entered Nirvâna, to reappear on earth in order to interfere on behalf of the faithful.

On the other hand, both ancient and modern philosophical schools of Buddhism have always had a leaning to and in most instances have actually defined Nirvâna as a state of absolute annihilation, where there is neither consciousness nor personality, nor existence of any kind. And I do believe that a consistent development of the principles of Buddhism must always lead to the same nagative result, that existence is but a curse and that therefore the aim of human effort should be the total annihilation of the personality and existence of each individual soul.

Modern philosophical schools of Buddhism are all more or less influenced by a spirit of sophistic nihilism. They deal with Nirvâna as they deal with every other dogma, with heaven and hell: they deny its objective reality, placing it altogether in the abstract. They dissolve every proposition into a thesis and its anti-thesis and deny both. Thus they say Nirvâna is not annihilation, but they also deny its positive odjective reality. According to them the soul enjoys in Nirvâna neither existence nor non-existence, it is neither eternal nor non-eternal, neither annihilated nor non-annihilated. Nirvâna is to them a state of which nothing can be said, to which no attributes can be given; it is altogether an abstract, devoid alike of all positive and all negative qualities.

What shall we say of such empty useless speculations, such sickly, dead words, whose fruitless sophistry offers to that natural yearning of the human heart after an eternal rest nothing better than—a philosophical myth? It is but natural that a religion which started with moral and intellectual bankruptcy should end in moral and intellectual suicide.

But sad, pitiably sad it is to see a religion that contains so many true ideas to produce results so barren, so deadly. Bunsen was right in his estimate of the value of this purposeless religion. Buddhism, he said, may be regarded as a sort of repose of humanity after its deliverance from the heavy yoke of Brahmanism and the wild orgies of nature worship. But this repose is that of a weary wanderer, who is withheld from the prosecution of God's work on this earth by his utter despair of the triumph of justice and truth in actual life. In the plan of the world's order it seems even now to be producing the effect of a mild dose of opium on the raving or despairing tribes of weary-hearted Asia.

The sleep lasts long, but it is a gentle one, and who knows how near may be the dawn of the resurrection morning?

LECTURE THE THIRD.

BUDDHISM, A POPULAR RELIGION.

In the preceding lecture I exhibited Buddhism from a doctrinal point of view. I endeavoured to do so with due impartiality, taking for my basis the more ancient scriptures of the Buddhists and confining my remarks to those features of doctrine, which are the common property of all the Buddhistic schools and sects. What is then the value of Buddhism as a system of doctrine?

No doubt Buddhism has brought to light many valuable and true ideas, and being free from any trammels of nationality it was peculiarly adapted to impress these truths upon all the peoples of Eastern Asia, among whom it obtained a footing. I have shown with what broad and enlarged views the Buddhists expounded that mysterious book of revelation, Nature, anticipating, centuries before Ptolemy, the latter's system of cycle and epicycle, orb in orb.

Though no Buddhist ever attained to the clearer insight and mathematical analysis of a Copernicus, Newton, Laplace or Herschel, it must be acknowledged that Buddhism fore-stalled in several instances the most splendid discoveries of modern astronomy. Teaching the origin of each world to have taken place out of a cloud, the Buddhists anticipated 2.000 years ago Herschel's nebular hypothesis. And when those very patches of cloudy light or diffused nebulosities which Herschel supposed to be "diffused matter hastening to a world birth" dissolved themselves before the monster telescope of Lord Rosse into as many assemblages of suns, into thousands of other world-systems dispersed through the wilds of boundless space, modern astronomy was but verifying the more ancient Buddhistic dogma of a plurality of worlds, of the co-existence of thousands of chiliocosmoi inhabited by multitudes of living beings.

Again, the Buddhist idea of each world being subject to destruction by fire, in order to be re-constructed again in a similar form, cannot be repugnant to modern astronomers, who witnessed the disappearance of stars through blazing conflagrations and who believe in the existence of a resisting medium in space, which retarding every year the movement of every planet and every sun finally results in the dissolution of every globe, to give way—as Buddhism teaches us—to a new heaven and a new earth.

Even some of the results of modern geology may be said to have been intuitively divined by Buddhism. For the Buddhists knew the interior of our earth to be in an incandescent state, they spoke of the formation of each earth as having occupied successive periods of incalculable duration, they strongly intimated that we are walking on the catacombs of dead generations, that we subsist on a world resting on worlds vanished.

Another spark of divine light which the Buddhists possessed is discernible in their recognizing and constantly teaching the most intimate connection between the visible and invisible world. They knew that "things seen are not the only realities." They looked upon the planets as inhabited by multitudes, all eagerly listening to Buddha's preaching. They peopled the air with spirits, the firmament with legions of human beings, superior to ourselves in purity and happiness, but constantly inter-communicating with us pigmies. They saw heaven open to each aspiring soul and mansions prepared there for those of a pure and tranquil heart. They understood that an immense crowd of spectators is watching us unseen with intense interest, a crowd of devils grinning with delight at the progress of evil, and hosts of angelic beings rejoicing over the spread of truth on earth.

The Buddhist system of morality also possesses, in spite of the many defects which I pointed out in the preceding lecture, many praiseworthy features. It started with the recognition of sin and evil as the heir-loom of mortal man. It pointed out in the strongest terms the impermanency and hollowness of everything earthly. It exhorted its devotees to extend love and charity to man and beast. It marked selfishness, lust and passion as the chief enemies of human happiness. It pointed out the superiority of the inward life over outward existence. It taught its adherents to look away from earthly sensual objects to regions invisible and inspired them—at least to a certain extent—with hopes of immortality.

On the other hand Buddhism is disfigured by some most important radical defects, which will in the estimation of an impartial critic far outweigh all the above mentioned points of advantage, and which in fact neutralize most of its beneficial elements. Whether we look upon Buddhism as a system of religion, morality or philosophy, we observe everywhere fundamental errors directly antagonistic to a healthly development of either the intellectual or moral faculties of mankind. But instead of repeating here all the detailed fallacies with which the Buddhist dogma is saturated and which I pointed out *en passant* in the preceding two lectures, it will suffice to give prominence to the most striking features, which mar the otherwise undeniable beauty of this grand system of natural religion.

Buddhism is intellectually defective. It arose from a feeling of spiritual bankruptcy and never after recovered its mental equilibrium. It is therefore essentially a religion of sullen despair, based on the total obliteration of a healthly faith in the actual constitution of things, penetrated by a spirit of morose *abandon*, mental and moral, and resulting in a barren sophistic nihilism which fails to recognize in nature, in history, in human affairs the will of God, and never thought of interpreting that will by the dictates of human conscience. Buddhism is in fact a system of religion without hope and strictly speaking even without God, a system of morality without a conscience, a system of philosophy which wears either the mask of transcendental mysticism or of nihilistic cynicism.

Again, Buddhism is further intellectually weak, because of its prodigious fondess for the miraculous, because it comes into collision with the results of experimental investigation and especially also because it gives such undue preference to the transcendental and the future, that it is utterly incapable of comprehending or appreciating the claims of reality and the demands of the present.

Morally also Buddhism is found sadly wanting. Though professing to destroy Self, its system of morality is pervaded by a spirit of calculating selfishness, its social virtues are essentially negative and strikingly unfruitful in good works.

Am I overstating my case and shooting beyond the mark? Is it that I prove too much and thus expose myself to the charge of having proved too little? Should not common sense tell me, that a religion so defective, so unnatural, so worthless, could not possibly have attained such wide-spread acceptation, could not have become the avowed creed of several hundred millions of reasoning creatures?

Certainly, if I had asserted that Buddhism remained anywhere or for any length of time a mere system of doctrine and consistently developed itself in practical life, as it was developed by thinking minds in the solitude of the cloister or in the study of the philosopher, I would have to demur to these charges. But the fact is, I have constantly kept in mind that Buddhism is one thing as a dogmatic theoretic system and another thing as a living practical religion, that Buddhism developed itself in one form under the crucible of logical thought and was moulded into another shape under the sober practical influences of daily life, in the struggle for existence.

Whilst the Buddhist philosopher or moralist in his study, in his pulpit, in his writings correctly unfolded Buddhism as a system of cold atheism and barren nihilism, the common people in all Buddhistic countries instinctively drifted into a form of worship essentially polytheistic and rose in some instances even to avowed Monotheism. Whilst the Buddhist philosophic canon (Abidharma) describes Nirvâna, the highest good of mankind, as a state of utter annihilation, the religious instincts of the people substituted for it hopes of more tangible positive beatitude. Whilst Buddhism as a system of doctrine leaves no room for the idea of atonement, the practical religious conscience asserted its divine rights and engrafted upon the ceremonial of the church a service of prayer and sacrifice especially intended to expiate the guilty conscience and to remove the consequences of sin and the sting of death and hell.

These are but instances, sufficient however to show that Goethe's famous saying

> "Ein guter Mensch in seinem dunkeln Drange
> Ist sich des rechten Weges wohl bewusst,"

so true and yet so simple, that it refuses to be translated, is as true in Asia as anywhere else.

We must allow therefore that unnatural and monstrous as Buddhism appears when viewed merely as a dogmatic system, many of its abnormities have been toned down, amended or rectified in the arena of practical life, under the influence of the religious conscience and common sense. It would be unjust then if I were to stop with the exposition of Buddhism on the basis of its canonical literature. It will be but fair to the reputation of Buddhism and necessary to the completion of this sketch of its religion, if I proceed to consider Buddhism as a practical religion, drawing my information from actual observation of modern Buddhistic worship as well as from the popular literature which circulates among the middle and lower classes of Buddhistic countries.

But to avoid useless repetitions I shall confine myself to those forms of religious belief and practice among modern Buddhists which deviate from the theoretical system of their own church.

It is a remnant of the ancient tree-worship, that almost every religious sect of Asia has a sacred tree of its own. The Brahmans revered the Ficus Indica, for which Buddhism originally substituted the Ficus Religiosa. But in course of time the Buddhists either reverted to the former tree or confounded the two. They were probably led to do so by the intuitive apprehension that Buddhism, as it grew and spread, singularly followed the mode of growth which is a distinctive mark of the sacred tree of the Brahmans, the Ficus Indica. It is a peculiarity of the latter that it extends itself by letting its branches droop and take root, planting nurseries of its own and so multiplying itself by that means, that a single tree forms a curiously arched grove.

This is precisely the way in which Buddhism propagated itself. It germinated in India, but sent out branches South and North, each taking root, and each perpetuating itself by further off-shoots, whilst the parent stock was gradually withering and finally decayed. Buddhism left but few traces behind in India, but it still lives in Ceylon and in the off-shoots of the Singhalese church in Burmah, Siam and Pegu. When Buddhism became almost totally extinct in India, the whole force of its vitality seemed to throw itself northwards and it spread with renewed vigour and widening shade over Cashmere, and Nepaul to China and Tibet. Chinese Buddhism threw forth new branches, northwards into Corea and Japan, and southwards over Cochin-China, Cambodia and Lagos, whilst Tibetan Buddhism pushed its branches into Mongolia, Manchuria and the greater part of Central Asia.

Now in each of these countries Buddhism established separate churches, each having its own locally diversified life, its own saplings, its own fruits and yet all these many branches with their endless ramifications form one grove, one compact whole, pervaded by the same sap, connected with each other and with the old withered parent stock in India by a net of intertwining roots.

It is quite beyond the limits of this lecture to go into all these national peculiarities and local varieties of Buddhism, interesting as they are to the student of comparative anthropology. I must confine myself to the more prominent general characteristics. And here we observe one grand distinction standing out in bold relief, a distinction which is now generally recognized by Buddhist scholars when they speak of Southern and Northern Buddhism.

Southern Buddhism, or the church of Ceylon with her offspring, being locally in close proximity to the parent stock and by natural circumstances in a comparatively isolated position, retained the strongest resemblance to the original Buddhism of India, and seemed sympathetically as it were to suffer under every blow struck at its parent stock. At first indeed Singhalese Buddhism displayed a vigorous healthy life: it spread to Burmah and Siam, and sent forth fresh shoots towards Sumatra, Java and Borneo. But the latter were nipped in the bud by the inroad of Mohammedanism which almost completely isolated the mother church in Ceylon and paralyzed her efforts. When Buddhism in India also received its death-blow the Singhalese church was still more affected by it. Its vigour and growth remained stunted ever after.

The consequence was that the Buddhist dogma was left in Ceylon, Burmah and Siam *in statu quo* up to the present day. There was too little life remaining for independent dogmatic and ecclesiastical development. There was little temptation from without to engraft foreign ideas and superstitions upon the traditional stock of doctrines and institutions. Shivaism and Shamanism, which saturated and leavened the Buddhist churches of the North to a very considerable extent, never influenced the minds of Southern Buddhists. They clung to the old traditions, retained the ancient dogma, preserved their primitive monastic and ecclesiatical forms in languid torpor, but with tolerable fidelity.

Still even here, Buddhism in getting popularized could not avoid altogether the modifying influences of the religious and moral instincts of the common people. What I said in the preceding lecture about Buddhism in general, substantially coincides with the theoretical teaching of modern Buddhists in Ceylon. But the common people there have instinctively toned down many of the unnatural products of Buddhistic scholasticism.

Cold, lifeless, abstract Atheism was too repulsive to the warm religious instincts and affections of the people who instinctively substituted for it idolatrous deification of humanity. They worship the seven ancient Buddhas, and Shâkyamuni Gâutama in particular, they accord divine honours to his principal disciples or Bôdhisattvas, they prostrate themselves before the images of these worthies, bring them offerings, address them in prayer, revere their relics with superstitious awe. But they do all this without making any logical distinction between the image and the heroe represented by it, without realising to themseves when they worship in the temples whether it is the mere act of worshipping that will avert calamity or procure happiness for them, or whether the invisible Buddha or Bôdhisattva actually has the power to influence their fortunes.

The educated Buddhist will always deny being guilty of idolatry. He merely remembers those ancient spiritual heroes by means of statuary representations, he merely vows in the presence of those idols to follow their example and practise morality and holiness. But the common people incapable of drawing such fine distinctions mechanically worship those heroes of their church, hoping thereby to derive temporal and eternal advantages. Theirs is therefore not an atheistic religion bnt a worship of the genius, a deification of humanity. And this is what Buddhism amounts to everywhere in the minds of the common people.

As the consciousness of God, this divine legacy inherited by every human soul, recoiled from the godless atheism of the metaphysician, thus also the sound common sense of the untutored multitude asserted itself in opposition to the refined teachings of the schools regarding the future state (Nirvâna). The literature of Southern Buddhism renounces the very idea of individuality, denies the existence of a separate ego, a self, and consistently therefore sees the highest boon of mankind in total annihilation of all forms of existence. Nirvâna is to this over-wise school-philosophy neither a state of consciousness nor unconsciousness, nor is it a state that is neither conscious nor unconscious: it is simply a non-entity, and the being that enters this state must become non-existent. This is what the Buddhist priest teaches to the present day; this is the food he offers to human souls hungering and thirsting for a future of happiness and bliss. Surely it is giving a stone to children crying for bread. And though it be the philosopher's stone, it is not to be wondered at if the common people turn away from it unsatisfied.

The fact is, this annihilation theory has nowhere in any Buddhistic country met with popular acceptation. Though Southern Buddhists did not proceed to substitute any definite conceptions of a real paradise of personal conscious immortality for this abstract metaphysical nihilism, they comforted themselves with the idea, that—whatever Nirvâna might actually be—there would be there no more of the horrors of transmigration, no more of the misery of life and death, no more of the torments of hell. Thus the common people accustomed themselves to think and speak of Nirvâna negatively. They understand it to be final cessation of the weary round of birth and death, a state absolutely exempt from all sorrows and troubles.

With the exception of these two points, Atheism and Nihilism, the practical religion of Southern Buddhists has adopted the whole range of Buddhist dogmas as exhibited in the preceding lecture. If we are to apply the historical distinction of Hinâyana and Mahâyana we might therefore consider Singhalese Buddhists to be followers of the Hinâyana system. When a learned Chinese Buddhist (Hiuentsang) who visited Ceylon in 640-45 A.D. classed the Buddhists of Ceylon among the adherents of the Mahâyana school, he had most probably before his mind those very points, the negation of Atheism and Nihilism, in which the practical religion of Southern Buddhists following the natural bent of the religious instincts and common sense assimilated itself, though unintentionally and independently, with their Northern contemporaries, among whom the Mahâyana school was then flourishing.

There are indeed a few other points of resemblance, instances of expansion given to original Buddhism by Buddhists of the North, types of which might be noticed in the popular Buddhism of Ceylon. If, for example, the common people of Ceylon—perhaps more or less unconsciously—bring their offerings to Buddhas and saints as if it were an atoning sacrifice, this might be looked upon as an expansion of the original Buddhism of India which indeed leaves no room for any atonement whatsoever, and as the germ from which the more elaborated ritual of propitiation and atonement now common among Northern Buddhists sprang. Minute investigation would also discover among modern Singhalese Buddhists slight traces of the Mysticism of the North.

These are, however, but minor points of resemblance, originating most likely not in any historical connection with the Mahâyana school of the North, but in the constitution and natural bent of the religious mind which is the same all the world over. The leading, ruling ideas in the practical religion of Singhalese Buddhism are not those of the Mahâyana school.

Taking all in all, therefore, I believe I am justified in saying that the Buddhism of Ceylon, even considered as a practical religion, has preserved more of the characteristics of primitive Buddhism than any other branch of the same church, and is on the whole a tolerably faithful exponent of that phase in the development of the Buddhist religion which is known under the name of the Hinâyana system.

The same might be said with some limitation of the Buddhist churches of Burmah and Siam, which are closely allied to the mother church of Ceylon and essentially belong to the same Hinâyana system, though they have used still more liberty in popularizing the traditional creed than the Singhalese ever ventured to do. Burmese and Siamese Buddhists were besides more than Singhalese Buddhists under the influence of Brahmanism and went even so far as to amalgamate with the Buddhist religion notions derived from the primitive tree and serpent worship which was a form of religion not only prior to Buddhism but indigenous in Burmah and Siam. The consequence is, that practical Buddhist worship there is marked by the prevalence of Brahmanic mythology.

As in Ceylon, so here also the scholastic system of nihilistic atheism has been converted into a popular form of polytheism, a worship of Buddhas and Bôdhisattvas, Nâgas and demons. There are moreover in Burmah and Siam many traces of the peculiar teachings and rites of the Mahâyana and even of the Tantra school, so that the popular Buddhism of these two countries may be considered to be the connecting link between the Buddhism of the South (Ceylon) and the Buddhists of the North (China, Tibet, &c.).

The religious systems of Northern Buddhism as carried out in practical life by the Buddhists of Cashmere, Nepaul, and all countries North and North-East of the Himalaya, will strike any observer at first sight as a most heterogeneous mixture of foreign, especially Indian, and native elements, embodying the mythological deities of almost any religion that ever existed in Eastern Asia.

Let us in imagination visit a Buddhist temple connected with a monastery, say the largest that is to be found in any of the above named regions, but which is only a magnified specimen of what you may find *en miniature* or in detached portions in every city within the sphere of Northern Buddhism. Let us also suppose that we have for our guide an intelligent and well-read Buddhist priest, a *rara avis* indeed, but still, let us charitably hope, to be found somewhere, one that is able to explain the mythological origin and meaning of all the objects of worship.

Start with him on your expedition, and he will point out to you a large tree marking from afar, as you approach, the locality of the sacred edifice, the gables of which are likewise remarkable from a distance by their peculiar shape and the dragon figures which surmount them. When your eye catches the splendid tree in front of the building, your guide will tell you that this tree is a specimen of the sacred Bôdhi-tree (Ficus religiosa), that an embassy expressly sent for this purpose to Buddha-gâya in India brought a shoot from the veritable tree under which Shâkyamuni sat when he attained to Buddhaship. You may remark that the tree before you is by no means a Ficus religiosa, but a Ficus indica, or it may happen that it is neither of the two, but a palm-tree (most probably then the Borassus flabelliformis); but the priest will tell you nevertheless with a bland smile that it *is* a Ficus religiosa, and that only ignorant and wantonly sceptical persons can have any doubt on the subject. Is there not a plate erected at the foot of the tree, stating that this tree grew out of a shoot brought directly from the holy land, cut off the very Bôdhi tree at Gâya?

As you turn towards the principal entrance of the building, you remark, a yard or two in advance of the flight of steps leading up to it, figures of crouching lions carved in stone and resting on pedestals, placed on either side. You will be told that these are emblems of Shâkyamuni whose cognomen Shâkyasimha (lit. Shâkya, the lion) indicates that he is by his moral excellence the king of men, as the lion by his strength is the king of the beasts. Perhaps your guide will even quote a passage from his sacred scriptures "as a lion's howl makes all animals tremble, subdues elephants, arrests birds in their flight and fish in the water, thus Buddha's utterances upset all other religions, subdue all devils, conquer all heretics and arrest all the misery of life."

If it is a sunny day you will find gathered on the entrance steps a motley assembly; priests and beggars, lying lazily in the sun, or engaged in entological pursuits, mending their clothes, cobbling their shoes, cleaning their opium pipes, smoking, gambling and so forth, and your appearance will be the signal for a general clamour for an alms offering in the shape of a foreign cent, or they will offer their services as guides. But if it should happen to be a feast day the steps and the whole open space in front, with the courtyards inside, will be crowded to excess by a busy multitude, men, women and children, who have come to worship or to consult the oracle, hawkers of fruit and other edibles, booths with fancy articles of all kinds, stalls opened by druggists, wandering doctors, fortune tellers, tents for the purpose of gambling, in short a complete fair which pushes its lumber and its clamour close to the very altars of the divinities worshipped inside the central temple.

As you enter the front-door, a martial figure with defying mien, armed to the teeth and sword in hand, confronts you. It is the image of Vêda, the patron and protector of monasteries. Inside the door there are to the right and left niches for the spirits of the door-way who are supposed to keep out all evil influences, and for the Nâga (dragon) spirits who are looked upon as the tutelary deities of the ground on which the sacred buildings are erected.

Having passed the first courtyard you are led through a second gateway, when your eye is arrested by four gigantic images, two being placed on either side of the gateway, guarding as it were with flaming eyes the entrance to the sanctuary beyond. Your guide will inform you that they are the demon-kings of the four regions (Tchatur Mahârâdjas) who guard the world against the attack of evil spirits (Asuras), that each of them is posted on a different side of the central mountain (Mêru) engaged in guarding and defending with the assistance of large armies under their command the corresponding quarter of the heavens. You will find incense lighted at the feet of these giants, and the images themselves almost covered with slips of paper containing either a record of vows to be performed in case of prayer answered by these heroes, or a record of thanks for favours already bestowed. For you will be told or may witness it perhaps with your own eyes, that these demon-kings are daily worshipped by the common people, who ascribe to them the power of healing all those diseases and of preventing or averting all those calamities which are supposed to be the work of evil spirits.

After crossing a second courtyard you reach the principal temple by ascending a small flight of steps. On entering this building you see before you five little altars placed in a row with a small image on each, and if it is the hour of prayer you may find a number of priests in full canonicals resembling so many Roman Catholic priests, chanting their monotonous litanies and responses to the sound of bell and a sort of wooden drum. The images before whom the priests every now and then prostrate themselves represent, as it may happen, either the five Celestial Buddhas (Vàirôchana, Akchôbhya, Amitâbha, Ratna Sambhava and Amôghasiddha) or their spiritual sons the so-called five celestial Bôdhisattvas (Samantabhadra, Vadjrapani, Ratnapani, Padmapani *i.e.*, Avalôkitêshvara or Kwanyin and Vishvapani). Your guide will explain to you that every historic Buddha may be viewed as possessing a triple form of existence, living or having lived among men on earth (Manuchi Buddha), existing metaphysically in Nirvâna (Dhyâni Buddha), and finally as a reflex of himself in a spiritual son generated in the world of forms for the purpose of propagating the religion established by him during his earthly career. He will further tell you by way of example that the famous founder of the present Buddhist Church was as Manuchi Buddha known under the name Shâkya-muni, as Dhyâni Buddha however he is called Amitâbha, whilst his reflex in the world of forms or, so to speak, his spiritual son is Padmapâni (Avalôkitêshvara). The five images therefore, before which you see the priests kneeling and prostrating themselves, all the while chanting their prayers, are the celestial types or the spiritual sons of those five ancient Buddhas who according to the general doctrine of Buddhism have already appeared in this present period (Kalpa).

Step nearer. You need not fear to give offence or to disturb the devotion of men, who, whilst mechanically continuing their monotonous litany and chanting their responses, will stretch out a hand to examine the texture of your clothes, to receive an alms, or offer to light your cigar or criticise in whispers the shape and size of your nose. Glance over the shoulder of one of those priests and examine his "manual of daily prayer." It is neatly printed in large-sized full-bodied native type and in the native character, but totally unintelligible to him, for it is Sanskrit, pure grammatical Sanskrit, systematically transliterated syllable by syllable. Listen to him, as he chants rythmically indeed but in drowsy monotonous voice: sarva tathâgatâ schamâm samâvasantu buddhyâ buddhyâ siddhyâ siddhyâ bodhaya bodhaya vibodhaya vibodhaya mochaya vimochaya vimochaya sodhaya sodhaya visodhaya visodhaya samantâm mochaya samanta, &c., &c. Poor fellow, he has not the slightest idea of the meaning of these words, though he may have been chanting these Sanskrit prayers day after day for ever so many years. But he has a notion that these strange sounds have some magic effect beneficial for himself and for the salvation of his soul. There is however tolerably good sense in the words of his prayer which reads, when translated, as follows: may all the Tathâgatas (i.e. Buddhas) take up their abode in me! ever teach, ever instruct, ever deliver with all knowledge! with all knowledge deliver, deliver, completely deliver! purify, purify, purify, completely purify! deliver, oh deliver all living creatures! &c., &c.

Pass on from these poor deluded souls that grope in the darkness for the light of a Saviour whom they know not. On the walls to the right and left you see ranged the life-sized statues of eighteen priests, Lohans or Arhans or Lamas your guide calls them. They also receive homage and worship by the priests who look upon them as the first apostles of Northern Buddhism.

But what do we see there in the background, partly screened by a large altar covered with censers and vases and plates of offering? Three colossal images, perhaps over thirty feet high, placed in sitting posture, carefully executed and richly gilt, their countenances bearing an expression of placid tranquility. Do not rashly jump at the conclusion that this must be a representation of the famous trinity of Northern Buddhists. Perhaps it is so, perhaps not. Appeal to your guide. If you are in a temple dedicated to the worship of Amitâbha Buddha, the triad of gigantic figures is Amitâbha in the centre, Avalôkitêshvara (his spiritual son) at his left, and Mahastamaprapta, a famous disciple of Buddha, at his right hand. Otherwise you may have before your eyes what are popularly—though not quite correctly—called the Buddhas of the past, present and future, that is to say, Shâkyamuni the historic founder of ancient Buddhism, Avalôkitêshvara (Kwanyin) the head of the present Buddhist hierarchy, who is however strictly speaking not a Buddha bnt a Bôdhisattva, and Mâitrêya the Buddha that is to appear in the future and is looked upon as the coming Messiah of Buddhism.

But suppose you have really before you the representation of the trinity, you will at once recognize the statue of Shâkyamuni Buddha by the curled hair and the curious bump on the top of his head. The second statue is conspicuous by four arms, two of which are folded in prayer whilst the third holds a rosary and the fourth a book: for this is the second person in the trinity, called Dharma (i.e. the law or religion). The third constituent of the trinity called Samgha (i.e. the church or clergy) is represented by a statue with two arms, of which the one rests on the knee, whilst the other holds a lotos-flower.

Well, you exclaim astonished, when your guide tells you that "these three are one," where has this dogma of a trinity come from? There is no trace of it in ancient or so to speak classic Buddhism. Southern Buddhists even to the present day know nothing of it. Where has it come from? Is it the Brahminical Trimurti of Brahma, Vishnu and Shiva, or is it perhaps an imitation of the Christian trinity of God the Father, the Son and the Holy Ghost? Neither of the two. The Brahminical Trimurti is in all probability of later growth than this Buddhistic Triratna. Besides there are no points of similarity in the offices ascribed to the individual constituents of the Buddhistic Triratna and the Brahminical Trimurti or the Christian trinity. The origin of this Buddhistic trinity is to be explained in this way.

It was natural that Shâkyamuni Gâutama Buddha, the great founder of Buddhism, should become an object of worship after his death. It was likewise natural, that when he was gone who had before been to his disciples the only criterion and judge of the truth, the followers of Buddhism should, in the absence of any standard work written by Shâkyamuni himself and in the absence of any fixed creed, feel the want of some comprehensive formula, some simple articles of faith, which might be to them what the *Confessio Apostolica* afterwards was to the early Christians.

In looking for such a short but comprehensive condensation of the faith established by Shâkyamuni, they naturally remembered first those of his sayings, which he had enunciated shortly before his death with the expressed intention of giving his disciples some guidance for the future. "Ananda," said he, "when I am gone, you must not think that there is no Buddha; the discourses I have delivered and the precepts I have enjoined must be my successors or representatives and be to you as Buddha." Well, there they had Buddha's discourses and precepts (*i.e.* Dharma) placed in the same rank with Buddha himself whom they already worshipped.

Again, among those "seven imperishable precepts" which Shâkyamuni gave to his disciples shortly before his death, the first in order is "to keep assemblies or convocations (Samgha) regularly from time to time." What can be more natural now, than that the first preachers of Buddhism after the removal of their great master used those three constituents Buddha, Dharma and Samgha as a standing theme for all their sermons, as the test of faith for those who wished to enter the Buddhist church?

At any rate it is an undisputed fact, that immediately after the death of Shâkyamuni the formula "I take my refuge in Buddha, Dharma and Samgha" was practically in use as the *formula fidei* for lay-members of the Buddhist church, and likewise that this very formula was commonly called the formula of "the three refuges" (Trisharana).

This then was apparently the starting point and the first stage in the process of development through which this Buddhist doctrine of a trinity passed. Had it stopped here—and Southern Buddhism never went farther—we could not speak of a trinity, but simply of a triple dogma, of a triad of articles of faith, of which the first inculcated the divine character of the founder of Buddhism as a person, whilst the second referred to the abstract unity of the Buddhist dogma, and the third to the collective unity of the clergy. All three were considered as worthy of reverence and divine worship, but they were not viewed as three persons nor as three persons in one, they formed no trinity.

In the course of time however this doctrine underwent some modification and received further development in the hands of Northern Buddhists and especially through the influence of the Mahâyana school. In this second period of the history of the Buddhist Triratna, the Brahminical Trimurti of Brahma, Vishnu and Shiva, *may* have influenced the speculative minds of Buddhist teachers. But even without assuming this to be the case, one may easily understand, how Buddhists of a speculative turn of mind might, without much impulse from without, by the mere impetus of speculative reasoning come to unite those three constituents or heads of doctrine and consider them as a threefold manifestation of one historical person (Shâkyamuni). They would then look upon Buddha as the personified intelligence, view his doctrine i.e. Dharma as the incarnate Logos and call Samgha (the Buddhist church or communion of saints) the collective unison of both. This at any rate is the form in which the idea of a Triratna was cast by the dogmatists of this period.

With the rise of the Tantra school ideas borrowed from Shivaism and mixed with Brahminical theories began to be freely transplanted upon the fruitful soil of Northern Buddhism. Shivaism, which ascribes to Shiva a threefold body, and Brahminism with its corresponding Trimurti of Brahma, Vishnu and Shiva gave now a fresh impetus to the development of the Buddhistic trinitarian dogma.

In Nepaul a threefold form of existence was ascribed to every Buddha, and the distinction, to which I alluded above, was made of a terrestrial Buddha

(Manuchi Buddha), of a celestial Buddha (Dhyâni Buddha) and of a reflex of the latter (Dhyâni Bôdhisattva).

In China and Tibet a similar distinction was made with regard to the nature of every Buddha. Intelligence (Bôdhi) being the fundamental characteristic of a Buddha, Northern Buddhists now distinguished (1) essence, (2) reflex, (3) practical application of his intelligence. Shâkyamuni was therefore considered to be personified intelligence, i.e. Buddha; his law or the religion established by him, his reflex, as it were, left behind when the man entered Nirvâna, was called Dharma; whilst the practical issue of both was said to be the church or rather the priesthood, which alone forms the church, and designated Samgha.

Now each of these three manifestations of one historical person received further the attributes of personality, and therefore to each a separate name was given. Buddha as a person retained of course his name Shâkyamuni; Dharma personified was called Vâirôtchana; and Samgha received the cognomen Lôchana. But these three persons were asserted to be essentially and substantially one.

Still the atheistic element in Buddhist speculation was too strong aud a reaction took place. Dharma was now placed in the first rank—to do away with the preponderance of the personal element,—and explained as the unconditioned underived entity, combining in itself the spiritual and material principles of the universe. . From Dharma, it was taught, proceeded Buddha by emanation as the creative energy, and produced in conjunction with Dharma the third constituent of the trinity, viz. Samgha, which was viewed as the comprehensive sum of all actual life or existence. Having thus destroyed the personal character of the first person (Dharma) in this trinity, Dharma was further identified with Pradjna, the highest virtue according to the Buddhist system of morality and the principal means for attaining to Nirvâna, implying especially a voluntary secession from the versatile phenomenal world into that of abstraction. Naturally then Dharma was viewed as an abstract first principle, Buddha became a mere phenomenon and Samgha an idea and nothing more. This is the form under which the so called Buddhist trinity is now-a-days promulgated among Northern Buddhists from Nepaul to Corea, even in popular literature. And this is, therefore, the meaning of the three colossal images, the sight of which has led us away into this lengthy digression. But, be it understood, this is the esoteric view of the Triratna.

The common people know little or nothing of such speculations. They see before them three separate deities, they speak of and worship not a triune god but a triad of idols, which they regard as three different divinities, totally ignoring their unity and unaware that the three "precious ones" they worship are after all but logical abstractions, a purely philosophical fiction.

But to return to realities, suppose you visit some of the smaller building, you will probably see in one of them a fine marble pagoda reaching to the very rafters of the roof. It is built in strict Indian style, tastefully decorated, and forms the receptacle of some sacred relic. There may be in it perhaps a hair of Buddha, or a tooth, or a particle of his robe, or some relic of one of his disciples. There also prayers are offered and sacrificial offerings of flowers, candles and incense presented by the people, who true to the fetichistic habits of their forefathers ascribe miraculous healing powers to such relics.

You pass on to another row of buildings containing several shrines. Conspicuous among them is the shrine of Amitâbha Buddha. A large crowd of people, chiefly men, are going through the usual forms of worship there, testifying to the great popularity of this deity. You notice on the breast of the idol a strange cross (the Svâstika). It is exactly the same diagram as that which you may have seen engraved on ancient church-bells in England and which learned antiquarians unanimously declare to be the hammer of Thor (the Scandinavian god of thunder). Perhaps also you remember to have heard that among the German peasantry and in Iceland the same figure is used as a magical charm to dispel thunder. Well, you turn to your guide. What is the meaning of this emblem? He informs you that it is the mystic shibboleth of the believers in the Western Paradise "an accumulation of lucky signs possessing ten thousand efficacies." But what about the Western Paradise?

The dogma of this paradise in the West, the Nirvâna of the common people, was (the tradition asserts) transmitted by Shâriputtra, one of the greatest disciples of Shâkyamuni. It is said that Buddha first told him of the existence of a land of extreme happiness (Sukhâvati), of a perfect paradise in the Far West, and gave in answer to Shâriputtra's questions the following particulars, which to the present day are generally believed in as gospel truth by Northern Buddhists.

In that paradise in the West, it is said, with its millions of Buddhas distributed over the country according to the eight points of the compass, there is one there discoursing on religion. His name is Amitâbha. He is so called because he is substantially light, boundless light, illuminating every part of his dominions. He is also of boundless age, immortal, and all his people are likewise enjoying immortality.

Now this paradise of the West, situated beyond the confines of our visible world, contains four precious things or wonders. In the first instance it is a kingdom of extreme happiness, there is there fulness of life, and no pain nor sorrow mixed with it, no need of being born again, no Nirvâna even. In the second instance there is there a seven-fold row of railings or balustrades, thirdly a seven-fold row of silken nets and lastly a seven-fold row of trees hedging in the whole country. In the midst of it there are seven precious ponds, the water of which possesses all the eight qualities which the best water can have, viz., it is still, it is pure and cold, it is sweet and agreeable, it is light and soft, it is fresh and rich, it tranquillizes, it removes hunger and thirst and finally it nourishes all roots. The bottom of these ponds is covered with gold sand, and round about there are pavements constructed of precious stones and metals, and many two-storied pavilions built of richly-coloured transparent jewels. On the surface of the water there are beautiful lotos-flowers floating, each as large as a carriage wheel, displaying the most dazzling colours, and dispersing the most fragrant aroma. There are also beautiful birds there which make delicious, enchanting music, and at every breath of wind the very trees on which those birds are resting join in the chorus, shaking their leaves in trembling accords of sweetest harmony. Those silken nets also which environ the whole paradise chime in. This music is like *Lieder ohne Worte*; its melodies speak to the heart; but they discourse on Buddha, Dharma and Samgha, and wake an echo in every breast, so that all the immortals that live in this happy land instinctively join in hymns of praise, devoutly invoking Buddha, Dharma and Samgha. But it is all the doing of the miraculous power of Amitâbha, who transforms himself into those birds, and produces those unearthly strains of heavenly music.

In this way the story goes on transplanting to this paradise in the West everything that an Asiatic considers beautiful and charming.

But it is remarkable what a pure moral atmosphere all the descriptions of this "pure land," as it is called, are breathing, for it is mentioned as one of the chief characteristics of this paradise, that no sin enters therein, no evil thought, no wickedness. All the inhabitants of it are pure and holy men. I say men, because there is no difference of sex there, but every woman, when born into the Western land, is at once transformed into a man. Another remarkable point in this dogma is, that the way by which one may obtain entrance into this paradise is exceedingly easy. For it is by no means absolutely necessary to renounce the world and to submit to ascetic austerities, celibacy and monastic rules, or to go through all the stages of abstract meditation and contemplation. What is absolutely required is merely an assiduous and devout worship of Amitâbha. "The very name of this Buddha, says a sacred text, if pronounced by a devout heart 1000 times or 5000 times, will effectually dispel all harassing thoughts, all fightings within and fears without. A continued sincere worship of Amitâbha will release men from the restless unceasing eddies of transmigration and bring them to the enjoyment of eternal peace and rest in the pure land of the Western heaven. And if once there, there will be no danger of being reborn again into the world of trouble and misery, or of having again to suffer the pangs of dying."

It is needless to remark, that this whole dogma, beautiful as it is in its conception, and a true response to the natural yearning of the human heart for an eternal Sabbath in heaven, is a flat contradiction to all the leading doctrines of Buddhism, granting as it does such an easy egress out of the Sansara and substituting immortality for the utter annihilation of the Nirvâna theory. But this leads us to the question, from what source did Northern Buddhists derive this strange medley? For it is another remarkable feature about this doctrine that the very name of Amitâbha and his paradise are perfectly unknown to the Buddhists of Ceylon, Burmah and Siam.

Strange to say, the dogma of Amitâbha made its first appearance in the literature of Northern Buddhism as early as 147 A.D., when a book under the name of Amitâbhasûtra was brought from the head-quarters of the Tochari Tartars (Cashmere) to China by a Cashmerian priest called Chi-lu-kia-ch'an. The next appearance of Amitâbha is in a list of 1000 Buddhas got up by the Mahâyana school. But it was not earlier than the fifth century that the worship of Amitâbha and the dogma of a paradise in the West began to spread largely.

The great Chinese traveller Fahien wandered (A. D. 400) all over India, but though he alludes to having noticed the worship of Avalôkitêshvara and Mandjushri, who are closely associated with the worship of Amitâbha, he never mentions the latter, and does not appear to have met in his travels with any trace of a worship addressed to Amitâbha. His countryman Hiuentsang, who (A.D. 629-45) passed through Central Asia and India, and published his observations in a very extensive and accurate form, is likewise silent on the subject.

Taking these circumstances together with the total absence of the dogma of Amitâbha, for which the Buddhist canon of Ceylon, Burmah and Siam is conspicuous, it seems evident, that India was not the birthplace of the worship of Amitâbha.

And now we may go a step farther. There is another circumstance which makes it probable that the dogma in question originated in Cashmere. It reached China in connection with that distinction of Dhyâni Buddhas and Dhyâni Bôdhisattvas and in connection with that before-mentioned list of 1000 Buddhas, both doctrines being a product of the Mahâyana school which was first got up in Cashmere and Nepaul.

Considering then that Amitâbha was originally conceived as impersonal, as the ideal representation of "boundless light,"—a significantly Gnostic idea,—remembering also that his name is mentioned in a list of 1000 Buddhas which naturally reminds us of the 1000 Zarathustras of the Persians, and taking finally into account that the whole doctrine of Amitâbha and his paradise in the "West" is not only unknown to Southern Buddhists, but diametrically opposed to the first principles of Buddhism, it seems most natural to seek the origin of this dogma in Gnostic or Persian ideas influencing the Buddhism of Cashmere and Nepaul.

Close to the shrine of Amitâbha you will find that of Avalôkitêshvara. As the former is especially worshipped by men whose spiritual watchword is "Westward-Ho," thus women throng round the altar of the latter in search of a guide to the promised Eldorado in the West. Examine the idol before you. It has the appearance of a female, with three faces joined to one head and a large number of arms, each grasping some symbol of doctrine or some weapon of defence.

May be, your guide informs you with the utmost gravity, that this idol has not been made by human hands but fell directly down from the clouds. There might be some sense in this statement if he referred to the dogma connected with the divinity which this idol represents. For, like the doctrine of Amitâbha, it does not seem to have come from the workshops of either Vêdic or Brahamanic mythology, nor does Southern Buddhism know of its origin.

And yet this Avalôkitéshvara—whose name is evidently Sanskrit—seems to have been largely worshipped in Northern and Central India a few centuries after the beginning of our era, and is at the present day the most popular deity of Northern Buddhists. Various names, titles and offices are given to this god—or goddess, for she is most commonly now represented as a woman. In China she is called Kwanyin (a literal translation of her Sanskrit name), in Japan she is known as Kwannon (a corruption of Kwanyin), whilst the Tibetans call her Cenresi and the Mongols Ergetu Khomsin. But all these names and all the legends connected with this deity express one and the same circle of ideas: that this divinity is the god or goddess "that has a thousand arms and a thousand eyes and a merciful heart," that she listens with compassion to the prayers of all who are in any distress of body or mind, especially however extending a saving hand to those who are in danger on the sea; that she is now the invisible head and ruler of the present Buddhist church, appearing now and then in the form of man or woman, to interfere on behalf of the faithful, to establish the doctrine of the paradise in the West, to save souls from hell, to assist in the propagation of Buddhism and so forth.

Many are the legends connected with this popular apostle of mercy. Avalôkitêshvara is first heard of as having resided at Pôtala, a port at the mouth of the Indus, the reputed home of Shâkyamuni's ancestors. Another Pôtala, likewise the scene of manifestations of Avalôkitêshvera's miraculous saving powers, is placed by the legend in "the South of India, East of the Malaya mountains in Malakuta," in other words somewhere on the coast of Malabar. When Simhala, an Indian Buddhist, was shipwrecked on the coast of Ceylon and ensnared by savage Sirens (Rakchasîs), Avalôkitêshvara appeared in the shape of a horse and carried him across the sea to India, whence he returned with an army, slew the Sirens and founded the kingdom of Ceylon, thenceforth the headquarters of Southern Buddhism.

In China, Avalôkitêshvara appeared as a woman, born under the name Kwanyin, as the third daughter of a (fabulous) king called Shubhavyuha (lit. Chwang-yen-wang), who—as the tradition, which identifies him with Chwang-wang of the Chow dynasty, boldly asserts,—lived about 696 B.C. Her father was an unbeliever and finding himself unable to overrule her objections against marriage, he allowed her to go into a convent, but by his orders she was there made to perform the most degrading offices for the other nuns. Celestial spirits (Richis) however came invisibly to do all the menial work for her. When her father found it out, he got so enraged that he set fire to the convent. But a rain fell and extinguished the fire and it appeared that no harm had been done to any of the 500 inmates. Thereupon the king ordered his daughter, Kwanyin, to be arrested and brought into court, but he secretly told her mother to coax the girl into submission. Kwanyin however remained stedfast: she would rather die than be married. The king then sent for the executioner and ordered him to cut off her head. But as often as the sword touched her neck, the blade split into a thousand pieces, without injuring her. The king now ordered her to be stifled with a red cloth. It was done, but a white tiger suddenly appeared and carried her body off to a dark forest. There her soul, being in a state of torpor, perceived a youth who waved a banner in his hands and ordered her to follow him into the presence of Yâma (the ruler of Hades). She followed him, but whilst passing through the various chambers of torture in hell she kept her hands folded, continually invoking Amitâbha Buddha. Thereupon a rain of flowers fell from heaven, the earth produced golden lotos-flowers, and all the instruments of torture used in hell were smashed. When she appeared before Yâma, the latter, seeing that hell changed under her footsteps into paradise, exclaimed in righteous indignation: how can the world be made better if we are to have no hell? So he ordered Kwanyin to be sent back to the dark forest whence she came. There she suddenly found herself awake as if from a dream. "I was in heaven," she exclaimed, "and yet here I find myself again on earth! Whither shall I go to dwell?" Whilst saying this she found herself confronted by a Buddhistic hermit, who invited her with many bland speeches to share his hermitage with him. Indignantly she refused this offer, reminding the hermit of Buddha's injunction that nuns and monks should live apart. But he replied, "I am Buddha himself and only came to test your virtue." He forthwith called a Nâga (dragon) spirit, who produced a large lotos-flower, invited her to sit on it, and thus conveyed her to the island of Pôtala on the China Coast (now called P'ootoo). There Kwanyin lived for nine years, saving many mariners from imminent peril and shipwreck, and healing the diseases of innumerable beings. Hearing that her father was dangerously ill, she cut all the flesh off her own arms, and made it into a medicine which restored him to health. To show his gratitude he ordered a statue of Kwanyin to be erected "with arms and eyes complete," but as the word "complete" has in Chinese the same sound (ts'ien) as the word for "thousand" (ts'ien), the two terms differing only in tone, the sculptor misunderstood the king's order. Thus it happened that a statue with "a thousand eyes and a thousand arms" perpetuated her memory.

The island of P'ootoo, where Kwanyin resided till her death, was in after times relieved from all taxes, handed over to the priesthood, and as the worship of Kwanyin spread over the whole of China and the neighbouring countries, this island continued to be and still is the object of veneration to which pious pilgrims resort from the farthest regions.

In Tibet also this deity manifested her glory. Avalôkitêshvara (as a male deity) is believed to be the ancestor of the Tibetan people. It is said that in ancient times he transformed himself into a monkey (Brasrinpo), and cohabiting with a demon, who for that purpose assumed the form of a female monkey (Brasrinmo or Khagroma), he became the father of three sons and three daughters. His children then peopled the previously uninhabited country of Tibet, and thus it has come to pass that the Tibetans, like true Darwinians, glory in their supposed descent from a monkey. Avalôkitêshvara afterwards exerted himself in various ways to spread the doctrines of Buddhism in Tibet, and it soon became an established custom there, to accord supreme spiritual and ecclesiastical jurisdiction to those only, who were considered to be incarnations of Avalôkitêshvara. Like the Chinese, the Tibetans also have their Pôtala, a mountain in Lhassa, on the top of which towers the residence of the Dalai Lama in whom and whose successors Avalôkitêshvara is supposed to be constantly incarnate.

Japan also has its "thousand-handed Kwannon," and the same is the case with all the other countries within the pale of Northern Buddhism, the legends there differing only through a slight local colouring from those current in China and elsewhere. One example will suffice. A Japanese tradition relates, that during the civil wars of the middle ages a political refugee, called Morihisa, hid himself in the temple of the thousand-handed Kwannon at Kiyomidzu in Kioto, and implored this deity with ceaseless prayers for a thousand days.. His enemies, however, discovered his retreat and dragged him out to the seashore for execution. But the executioner found all his efforts foiled by the God Kwannon, for at every stroke he essayed, the sword blade split into a thousand pieces without injuring Morihisa. His enemy, who had previously slain all the other members of Morihisa's clan, received also a warning through his own wife, to whom Kwannon had appeared in a dream interceding on behalf of Morihisa. The latter was therefore set at liberty and being the acknowledged protegé of Kwannon he rose to the highest power in the state.

It is impossible to say where and by whom this dogma of Avalôkitêshvara was got up. Judging from internal evidences it would appear that it was first developed by the Mahâyana school. This school gave Avalôkitêshvara even a place in the trinity, uniting him (her) as the personification of love and charity with another fictitious Bôdhisattva, called Mandjushrî, the apotheosis of transcendental wisdom, and with Vadjrapâni, the Indra of the Vêdas, now looked upon as the god of thunder and the personification of power. Forming one of the constituents of the trinity, Avalôkitêshvara received the title Ishvara (Lord), and for the same reason it is that he (she) is often represented with three faces or with eleven faces arranged in three divisions.

Afterwards the Tantra school applied its idea of Celestial Buddhas and Bôdhisattvas upon this dogma and Avalôkitêshvara was then declared to be the spiritual reflex or son of Amitâbha Buddha.

Shivaism also had its influence upon the formation of the dogma in question, and Avalôkitêshvara is consequently often represented with three eyes, with a crown of skulls on her head or a necklace of skulls or a rosary made of finger bones. Shivaism especially promoted Avalôkitêshvara's being viewed as a female deity endowed with great powers of sorcery and as the authoress of a most popular magic formula, "om mani padme hum", which is used by all Northern Buddhists as a favourite formula of exorcism or inscribed on amulets, on houses, walls, pillars, books, pill-boxes, coins and so forth, being supposed to be the most effective charm against calamities and noxious influences of all kinds.

I have gone into all these legendary accounts current among the people with reference to this particular deity, because they form a fair specimen of the popular hagiology of Northern Buddhists. Similar stories are told about many other minor deities, whose effigies you will find profusely scattered over the many courts and chapels connected with any large temple. Most of them bear names which connect their origin and history with Brahmanic or even Védic mythology. Many however of these *dii minores* are purely deifications of ancient native worthies. Famous priests, physicians of great renown, women of extraordinary devotion, munificence and piety, have been honoured with a place in the popular pantheon, and are as devoutly worshipped in their native countries as any of the ancient Buddhas and Bôdhisattvas.

But suppose you retrace your steps through the various temples you have visited, you will find it interesting to have a look at the apartments occupied by the priests. They have most of them their own cells, but dine together in one large hall, which, together with the kitchen and its enormous rice-boilers, are worthy a visit. The abbot has his private rooms apart from the cells of the priests. You may find him willing to receive you, but you will be astonished if you enter his rooms, expecting to find there the same primitive simplicity and economy, which you noticed when passing through the apartments allotted to the use of the priests, and which reminded you so strongly of the internal arrangements of a Roman Catholic monastery. A modern abbot takes it generally very easy. If his monastery is not too far from any centre of foreign commerce, he will show you with pride a collection of articles *de luxe*. He has watches and clocks of foreign manufacture, photographs of less than questionable decency, and he is generally not only a confirmed opium smoker, but considers himself a good judge of champagne, port and sherry. His attendants are invariably laymen, relatives of his own, who may have no intention whatever to take the vows. But the same abbot may also have a printing press with moveable types, likewise of foreign manufacture, and you may see it turning out neat reprints of the most popular portions of the Buddhist scriptures, or little tracts and pamphlets of local reputation.

After a visit to the gardens, which are generally well kept and abound in curious specimens of artificial training, after a passing glance at the place where the bodies of deceased priests are burned and the tomb which covers their ashes, you return through the labyrinth of galleries and courts. In one of the latter you may now notice a series of little chambers, popularly called chambers of horrors, containing statuary representations of the various tortures supposed to be employed in the various compartments of hell. For your guide will tell you, with a sly hit at yourself, that all those, who do not believe in Buddhism or violate its commandments, will after death be reborn in hell. He will inform you that there are underneath our earth eight large hells of extreme heat, eight more of extreme cold, again eight hells of utter darkness, and on the edge of each universe ten cold hells, but as each of these hells has many antechambers and smaller hells attached, all being places of torture, there are in reality altogether over a hundred thousand of such chambers of horrors. A pleasant prospect to heretics like yourself,—your priest will add.

Whilst Southern Buddhists knew only eight principal hells of extreme heat and minor hells on the extreme border of each universe, Northern Buddhists added the above-mentioned cold hells and beside those a special hell for females, called the placenta-tank, which is believed to consist of an immense pool of blood, and from this hell it is said no release is possible. Poor women, Buddhism does not seem to appreciate the rights nor even the goodness of women. All the other hells, with the exception of this female apartment, are only purgatories, and release from them can be procured through good works or through the atoning masses performed by the priests on behalf of the sufferers in hell.

On passing out through the gate, your eye may perhaps be arrested by a crowd of people surrounding a number of pigs wallowing in the richest food thrown before them. You will also notice in a conspicuous position near these pigs a poor-box, into which the people drop their offerings of money. What is it all about? Look at the inscription affixed to that box in large staring letters "save life!" The greatest Buddhist commandment is that which forbids the taking of life. All life, human as well as animal life, is absolutely sacred in the eyes of the Buddhist devotee. The killing of animals for the purpose of food is a heinous offence. Still more so is the love of cruelty which leads the strong to prey upon the weak and enables the sportsman, the fox-hunter, the deer-stalker, the pigeon-shooter in heathen and Christian countries to derive a horrible enjoyment from the piteous sufferings of poor dumb animals. Those pigs are therefore exhibited by the priests to remind the people of this greatest of all Buddhist commandments. And the people drop their mites into the box by way of atoning to some extent for their own shortcomings in that respect. For Northern Buddhists are—with the exception of the priests—by no means vegetarians, and even priests may be seen privately enjoying the good things of this world in the shape of animal food. Still I should think you will be inclined to bestow some praise on these pious priests who charitably feed those "sacred pigs," as European travellers have styled them, for the mere respect of animal life, who interpret the command "thou shalt love thy neighbour as thyself" in a wider sense even than Christian, and see their neighburs not only in their fellowmen, but also in every single member of the animal world, in every wild beast and even in the despised pig that wallows in the mud. And certainly a public protest against cruel sports and useless destruction of animal life is a good and needful thing, for sports of a cruel character do tend to blunt the feelings and develop that terrible callousness of disposition which leads to an utter disregard of the sanctity of human life. But, on the other hand, it is ridiculous to compare this Buddhist commandment "thou shalt not take life" with the religion of Him who would not break the bruised reed nor quench the smoking flax, and to give the palm—as some European admirers of Buddhism have actually done—to this Buddhist ideal of charity. Just ask your guide whether the Buddhist church, which so laudably extends its charity even to the brute creation and assiduously feeds sacred pigs in its monasteries, exerts herself to ameliorate the condition of poor suffering humanity? He will have to acknowledge that no hospitals, no asylums for the blind, the deformed, the destitute, have ever been founded by a Buddhist community. Alms, indeed, are encouraged, but they are to be bestowed on the worthiest, on the priest, the cloister, the church, and thus the current of charity is diverted from the destitute or outcasts of society whose very destitution is according to the Buddhist scriptures a proof of their unworthiness, to the worthiest on earth, to the community of priests, who are bound to receive the gifts bestowed, in order that the faithful may acquire merit, though forbidden by the self-renouncing principles of their creed to retain them for their private advantage. Thus it was brought about that the Buddhist priests take to feeding sacred pigs. A Buddhist

Peabody, therefore, would be doing the correct thing if he were to throw all his humanitarian efforts with all his money—before the swine.

It is almost needless to remark after the above-given explanations that those "sacred pigs" receive nowhere in any Buddhistic country anything like worship either by the people or by the priests. And yet a member of the American Expedition to China and Japan fell into this error and published it abroad in the printed report of that expedition. After describing what he calls the sacred pigs in the sacred styes in Canton, he exclaims in pitiful tone, "It was something of a curiosity though somewhat saddening in the reflections it occasioned to behold the sanctified pork and the reverence with which it is worshipped." I would not have mentioned this absurd mistake had not a learned writer in the *Fortnightly Review* (Feb., 1870, p. 215) based on this misconception a whole system of pig-worship and pages of lucubrations about "the primitive mysterious boar' who "is worshipped in China and was worshipped among the Celts," and placed that supposed pig-worship of China into analogy with "the existing worship of Vishnu in his avatar as a boar." There is no people in the world fonder of pork than the Chinese are, but there is not a trace of porcine-worship to be found among them, unless the "worship of the pig" consists in eating it.

Well, you have visited a fair specimen of the popular pantheon of Northern Buddhism. What is the result? You have seen multitudes of men and women bowing down before idols of clay, offering their gifts, addressing them in words of prayer and praise and thanksgiving, consulting the oracle by throwing lots in their presence and receiving a slip of paper issued in the name of the individual deity in the ambiguous terms of Delphi; you have noticed the reverence, the trust, the fervour with which—not the priests indeed—but the common people appeal to these legions of gods.

Is this the boasted Atheism of the Buddhist religion? Surely many, even of the common people, may be able to distinguish the idol from the divinity it represents, but it is undeniable that even they have before their minds during the act of worship the idea of a personal being of great power, mighty to save, to bless, to avert misfortune. From the legends connected with the several deities worshipped by the people it appears that they all were originally human beings. Though they now appear clothed in supernatural garb, heavenly spirits, genii, demons, they all are believed to have been human beings, plain men or women, at some time or other. And yet the very names Buddha, Bôdhisattva, Arhat, which once signified but moral fallible men more or less advanced in the path to Nirvâna, have in the parlance of the multitude in Buddhistic communities assumed a far higher significance. Buddha is to them simply the highest God, the *Deus optimus maximus.* Bôdhisattvas (and Arhats) are demi-gods. The former is God in *esse*, the latter are gods in *posse.* Both, Buddhas and Bôdhisattvas, are worshipped and relied on as God by Northern Buddhists. The difference lies in this, that Buddhas are looked upon as highest in rank, whilst Bôdhisattvas are considered to be nearest in sympathy. So then, as there are many Buddhas and many Bôdhisattvas, the religion of Northern Buddhists is practically systematic deification of humanity, displayed in a thoroughly polytheistic form of worship.

But in many instances these polytheistic practices have been developed into a form of religion very much akin to Monotheism. Nepaul for instance has one supreme Buddha, called Adi-Buddha. Several European scholars (Hodgson, and after him Bunsen and others) have taken hold of this fact and triumphantly proclaimed abroad, that Buddhism so far from being a system of Atheism had led its devotees (in Nepaul at least) to direct Monotheism.

This assertion however requires some modification. If we examine the facts of the case, we find that the term Adi-Buddha means simply "an ancient Buddha" and that the Nepaulese like all other Buddhists know not less than seven ancient Buddhas. Still it is true that Nepaulese Buddhists—like all Northern Buddhists who are under the influence of the Mahâyana school—show a decided preference for one of these ancient worthies or rather for his celestial form (Dhyâni Buddha), and this celestial Buddha is then styled Adi-Buddha *par excellence.* Indeed they address him and worship him very much as if he were a supreme god, but theoretically speaking his personality is lost in philosophical abstractions which identify this Adi-Buddha with the highest moral virtue (Pradjnâ), and convert him into a mere hyperbole, a mere figure of speech expressing the existence of a moral law in the universe. Strictly speaking they do not look upon him as the personal creator and sustainer of the universe. And yet it is undeniable that there is at the bottom of this Adi-Buddha theory a strong tendency towards Monotheism, which though counteracted by philosophical scholasticism, shows itself in the popularized form of this dogma of one Adi-Buddha.

The common people of Nepaul reverence and pray to this Buddha in decided preference to all other Buddhas. They rely upon him for protection and salvation, treating him to all practical intents and purposes as if he were the highest God, a personal being of unlimited wisdom, goodness and power, the very creator and sustainer of the world. What Âdi Buddha is to the Nepaulese the same is the above-mentioned Amitâbha Buddha, with his spiritual progeny (Avalôkitêshvara), to the majority of Northern Buddhists. When they come to reason on the subject they indeed allow that he is not the first cause of the existence of the universe, tha the is but the regent of the far-famed paradise in the West, and yet practically they implore him, or his vice-gerent Avalôkitêshvara, as if he were Almighty God, creator and ruler of the whole world, omniscient, omnipresent. Though sceptic philosophers may treat this dogma as a mere allegory, the common people stoutly maintain their belief in Amitâbha as the highest personal God, and in the objective reality of his paradise.

We see therefore in this popular belief in an Adi-Buddha or Amitâbha the instinctive groping of the religious conscience after the unknown God, a faint glimmering of the truth which revelation alone can bring home to the human mind in full undimmed clearness. The same is the case with that popular legend of a paradise in the western regions: it is a spark of divine light, a particle of the truth which Christianity alone has unfolded in the revelation of a heavenly Jerusalem, where there shall be no more death, neither sorrow nor crying, for the former things have passed away.

There is another point in which the religious conscience of Northern Buddhists, unsatisfied by ancient Buddhism, added to the inherited traditional stock of ideas. Ancient Buddhism knows of no sin-atoning power; it holds out to the troubled guilty conscience no prospect of mercy, no chance of obtaining forgiveness, no possibility of justification, allowing not even so much as extenuation of guilt under any circumstances whatever.

A Buddha is not a Saviour. The only thing he can do for others is to show them the way of doing good and overcoming evil, to point out the path to Nirvâna by his example, and to encourage others by means of teaching and exhortation and warning to follow his footsteps. If any human being is to reach Nirvâna it must be done by independent action. Do good and you will be saved,—this is the long and short of the Buddhist religion. The sinner must expiate his guilt by punishment and by redoubled exertions in good works. There is indeed a ceremony of confession of sins,—for the priest; but it only serves to set him right again in his relation to the community of priests; it does not influence his prospects of future happiness.

Buddhism therefore is the hardest of all laws, for it blesses indeed the righteous, but it curses and condemns the sinner without extending a helping hand, without promising any pardon to any repenting contrite heart. There is a Nirvâna for the virtuous and innumerable hells are there for the wicked, and nothing more. Every individual has to work out his own salvation, unaided, unpitied, uncared for, placed between heaven and hell, trembling under the unrelenting yoke of the moral law of his religion—naturally a burden too heavy to be borne.

We have already seen how the common people endeavour to propitiate the gods of their own making by sacrificial offerings, supposing thereby to obtain in spite of their own shortcomings the favour of these deities. We have further seen how the same power was attributed to prayer, to a mere invocation of the names of certain deities or the mere recital of short forms of prayer believed to have been invented by them. These mystic formulae, invariably couched in Sanskrit, were popularly trusted in, being supposed to possess magic sin-atoning and saving powers. The very circumstance of their being constituted by the unintelligible sounds of a foreign language inspired the people with so much more awe and confidence. *Omne ignotum pro mirabile est.* Foremost among these magic sounds ranks the triliteral monosyllable om (or aum), the symbol of the trinity, the I am that I am, the alpha and omega of Northern Buddhism.

Of course this state of things could not be endured by a clergy fond of wielding uncontrolled power over the multitude. The priests had foresight enough to understand that the power of prayer, if freely accessible to all, would diminish their influence upon the people. It was an encroachment upon their privileges. As however the *vox populi*—in this case something like *vox Dei*—was too strong to resist it with any hope of success, they adopted the idea of atonement through prayer, but took it into their own keeping, establishing an elaborate ritual for the purpose of expiating guilt, counteracting evil influences of all sorts, alleviating the tortures of hell, procuring release from hell and re-birth into one of the heavens or into the Western Paradise. To engraft this ritual upon the orthodox tradition, to prove that it was in perfect accordance with the principles of ancient Buddhism, they produced a most voluminous literature (Yôgatchara Sûtras and Dhâranis) on the subject, ingeniously forging whole Sûtras composed in ancient style and making Shâkyamuni himself therein enunciate those ideas of an atonement procurable through the intercession of the priests.

Thus they established a ritual for the purpose under the pretended authority of Shâkyamuni. But the ritual in question is so richly interlarded with Sanskrit prayers, and the ceremonies prescribed in it are so complicated and surrounded with so much hocus-pocus, that it not only imposed upon the common people who were appalled by the assumed halo of ancient authority and listened with superstitious fear and reverence to the mystic jargon the very obscurity of which made them consider it profound, but it made the whole ceremonial a monopoly of the priests. For they alone have the key to the understanding of the whole, they alone can teach its mechanical details.

Quite a number of magic paraphernalia, the handling of which remains a mystery to the uninitiated, is necessary for the proper performance of that ritual. There is the so-called sceptre of Indra (Vadjra) used as a magic wand for the purpose of mantic conjurations and exorcism, there are magic circles and mystic diagrams to be drawn, holy water to be consecrated and sprinkled about, rice and flowers to be scattered to the rythmic recital of magic incantations (in Sanskrit), whilst the officiating priest goes through certain stages of ecstatic meditation in order to identify himself with the particular deity invoked in each case and accompanies the prayers of the priests by mysterious manipulations (Mudrâ).

To give an idea of the latter I will but quote a passage or two from a commentary to one of those rituals. "The officiating priest has in his heart, pronounces with his mouth and imitates with his fingers the mystic (Sanskrit) character hri, whereupon from his heart, mouth and fingers proceed rays of red-coloured light which destroy hell (s.c. for the benefit of those individuals on behalf of whom the ritual is gone through)." Again we read in the same work, "the officiating priest, lifting up the middle-finger of each hand and pressing both hands close together forms the sign hri whereupon from the points of his middle fingers a stream of mercy goes out which takes away the sins and guilt of all evil-doers." It is needless to add that this ritual intended especially for the benefit of the souls of deceased persons and in that case accompanied by the burning of many utensils and articles of luxury, all made of paper, is only performed in return for a certain sum of money paid to the priests, and that the length and consequent efficacy of the ceremonial gone through on behalf of any individual depends upon the length of the latter's purse.

* * *

This then is the practical religion of Northern Buddhism, or rather, I should say, this is what classic Buddhism has come to in the hands of the common people.

I take leave of my subject, which I make bold to say, I have endeavoured to elucidate honestly and impartially. I have striven to do justice to everything that is good and true in Buddhism. But in the interest of truth I have to confess, and I trust the above given facts will bear me out in the assertion, that Buddhism is after all neither better nor worse than any other religion built up by man: it is a science without inspiration, a religion without God, a body without a spirit, unable to regenerate, cheerless, cold, dead and deplorably barren of results. Can these dry bones live?

FINIS.